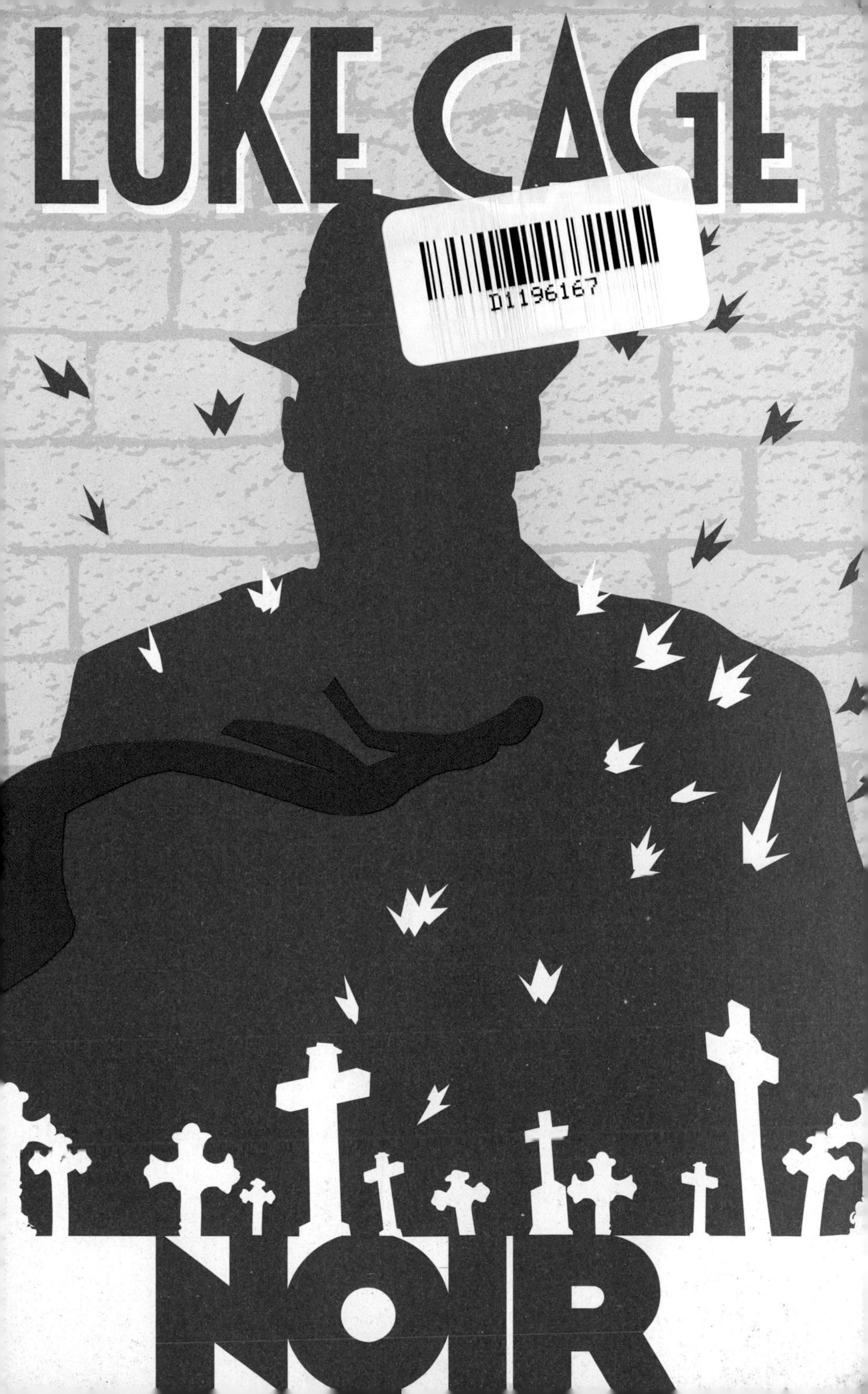
LUKE CAGE
NOIR

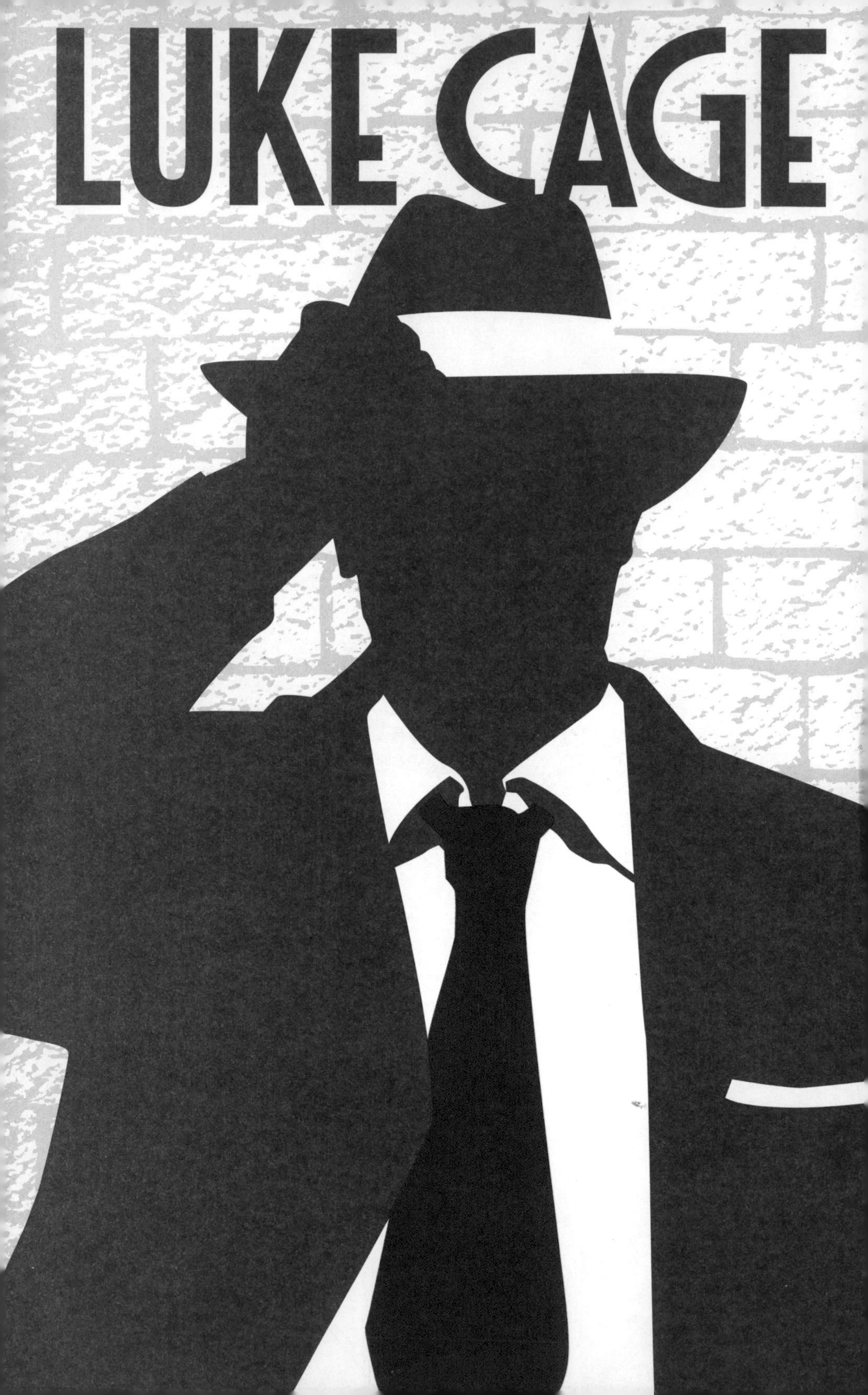
LUKE CAGE

GN BEN

WRITERS
MIKE BENSON
& ADAM GLASS

ART
SHAWN MARTINBROUGH

COLORIST
NICK FILARDI

LETTERER
VC'S CORY PETIT

COVER ARTIST
TIM BRADSTREET

ASSISTANT EDITOR
SEBASTIAN GIRNER

EDITOR
AXEL ALONSO

COLLECTION EDITOR
JENNIFER GRÜNWALD
ASSISTANT EDITORS
ALEX STARBUCK & JOHN DENNING
EDITOR, SPECIAL PROJECTS
MARK D. BEAZLEY
SENIOR EDITOR, SPECIAL PROJECTS
JEFF YOUNGQUIST
SENIOR VICE PRESIDENT OF SALES
DAVID GABRIEL
BOOK DESIGN
JEFF POWELL

EDITOR IN CHIEF
JOE QUESADA
PUBLISHER
DAN BUCKLEY
EXECUTIVE PRODUCER
ALAN FINE

LUKE CAGE NOIR. Contains material originally published in magazine form as LUKE CAGE NOIR #1-4. First printing 2010. ISBN# 978-0-7851-3545-6. Published by MARVEL WORLDWIDE, INC., a subsidiary of MARVEL ENTERTAINMENT, LLC. OFFICE OF PUBLICATION: 417 5th Avenue, New York, NY 10016. Copyright © 2009 and 2010 Marvel Characters, Inc. All rights reserved. $14.99 per copy in the U.S. and $16.99 in Canada (GST #R127032852); Canadian Agreement #40668537. All characters featured in this issue and the distinctive names and likenesses thereof, and all related indicia are trademarks of Marvel Characters, Inc. No similarity between any of the names, characters, persons, and/or institutions in this magazine with those of any living or dead person or institution is intended, and any such similarity which may exist is purely coincidental. **Printed in the U.S.A.** ALAN FINE, EVP - Office of the President, Marvel Worldwide, Inc. and EVP & CMO Marvel Characters B.V.; DAN BUCKLEY, Chief Executive Officer and Publisher - Print, Animation & Digital Media; JIM SOKOLOWSKI, Chief Operating Officer; DAVID GABRIEL, SVP of Publishing Sales & Circulation; DAVID BOGART, SVP of Business Affairs & Talent Management; MICHAEL PASCIULLO, VP Merchandising & Communications; JIM O'KEEFE, VP of Operations & Logistics; DAN CARR, Executive Director of Publishing Technology; JUSTIN F. GABRIE, Director of Publishing & Editorial Operations; SUSAN CRESPI, Editorial Operations Manager; ALEX MORALES, Publishing Operations Manager; STAN LEE, Chairman Emeritus. For information regarding advertising in Marvel Comics or on Marvel.com, please contact Ron Stern, VP of Business Development, at rstern@marvel.com. For Marvel subscription inquiries, please call 800-217-9158. **Manufactured between 7/2/10 and 7/21/10 by R.R. DONNELLEY, INC. (CRAWFORD), CRAWFORDSVILLE, IN, USA.**

10 9 8 7 6 5 4 3 2 1

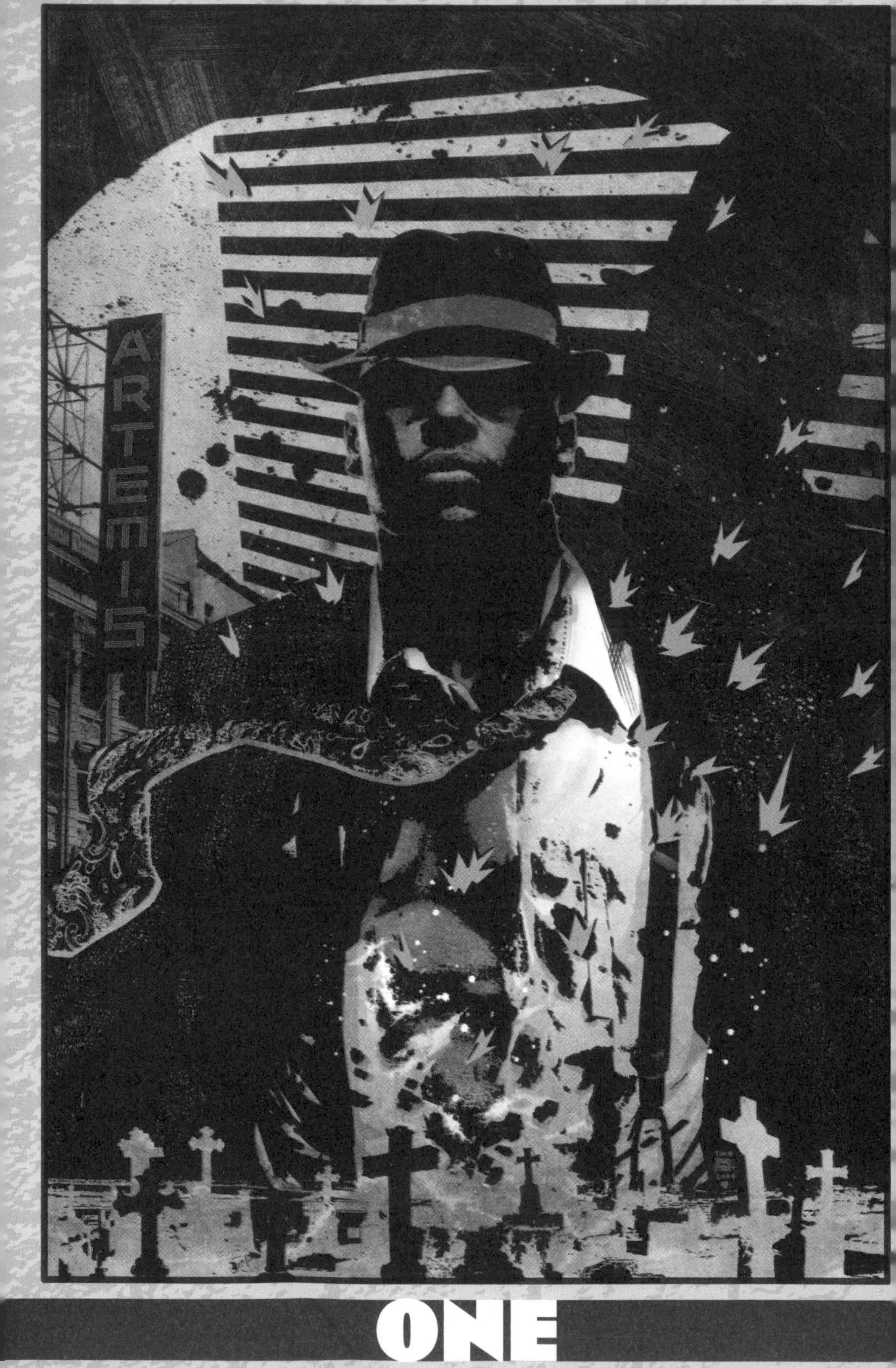
ARTEMIS

ONE

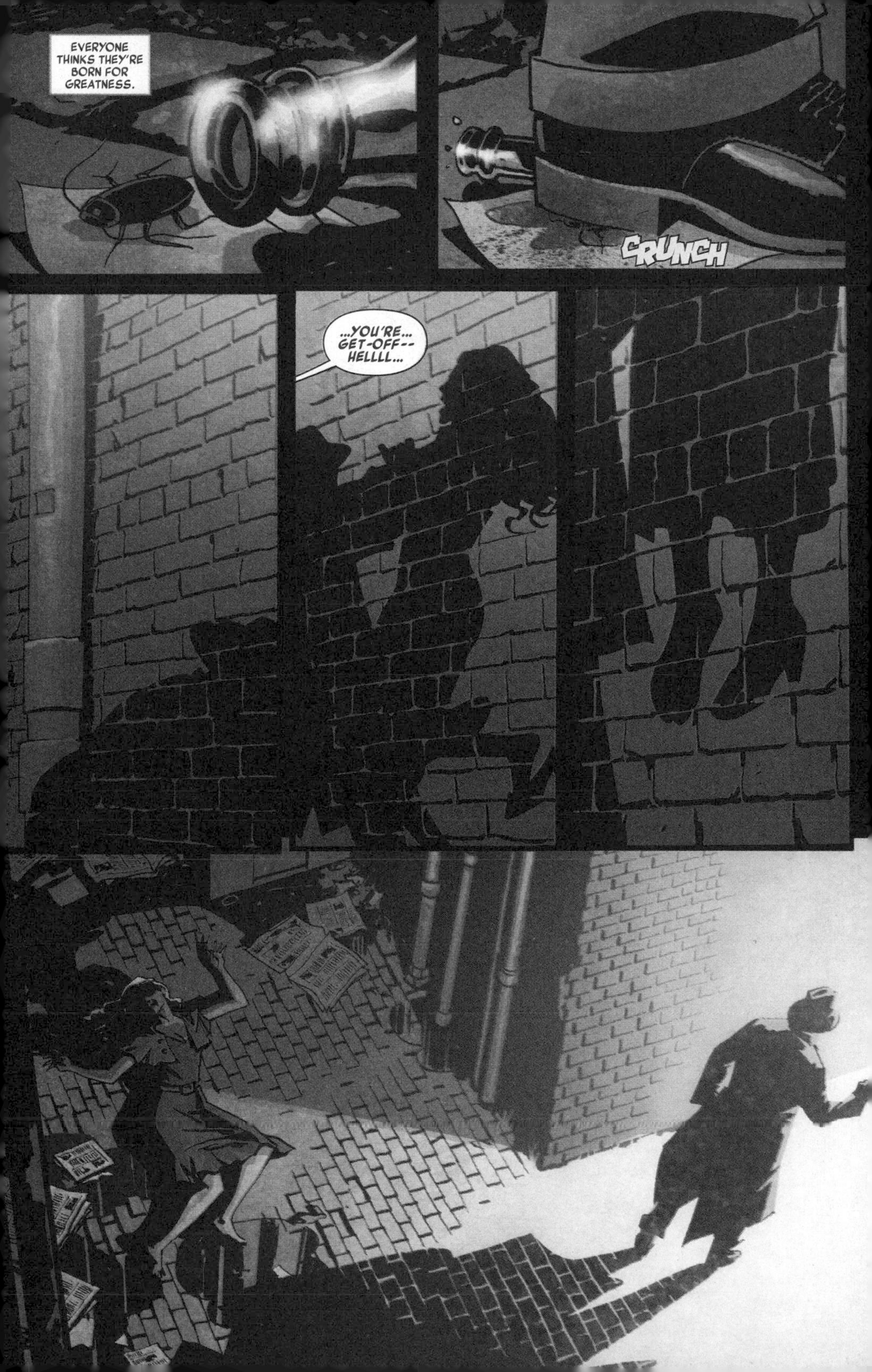
EVERYONE THINKS THEY'RE BORN FOR GREATNESS.
CRUNCH
...YOU'RE... GET-OFF-- HELLLL...

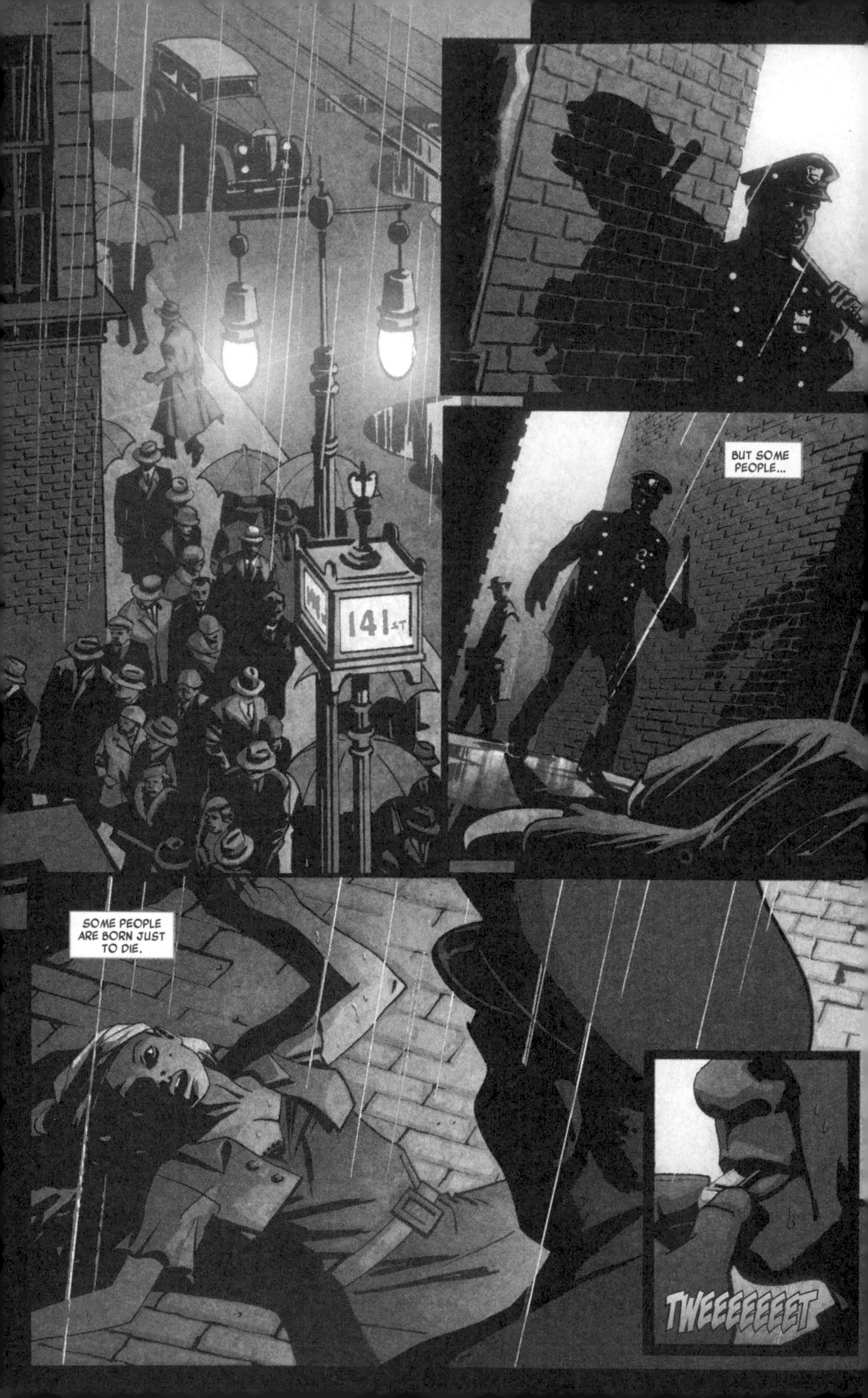
141 ST
BUT SOME PEOPLE...
SOME PEOPLE ARE BORN JUST TO DIE.
TWEEEEEEET

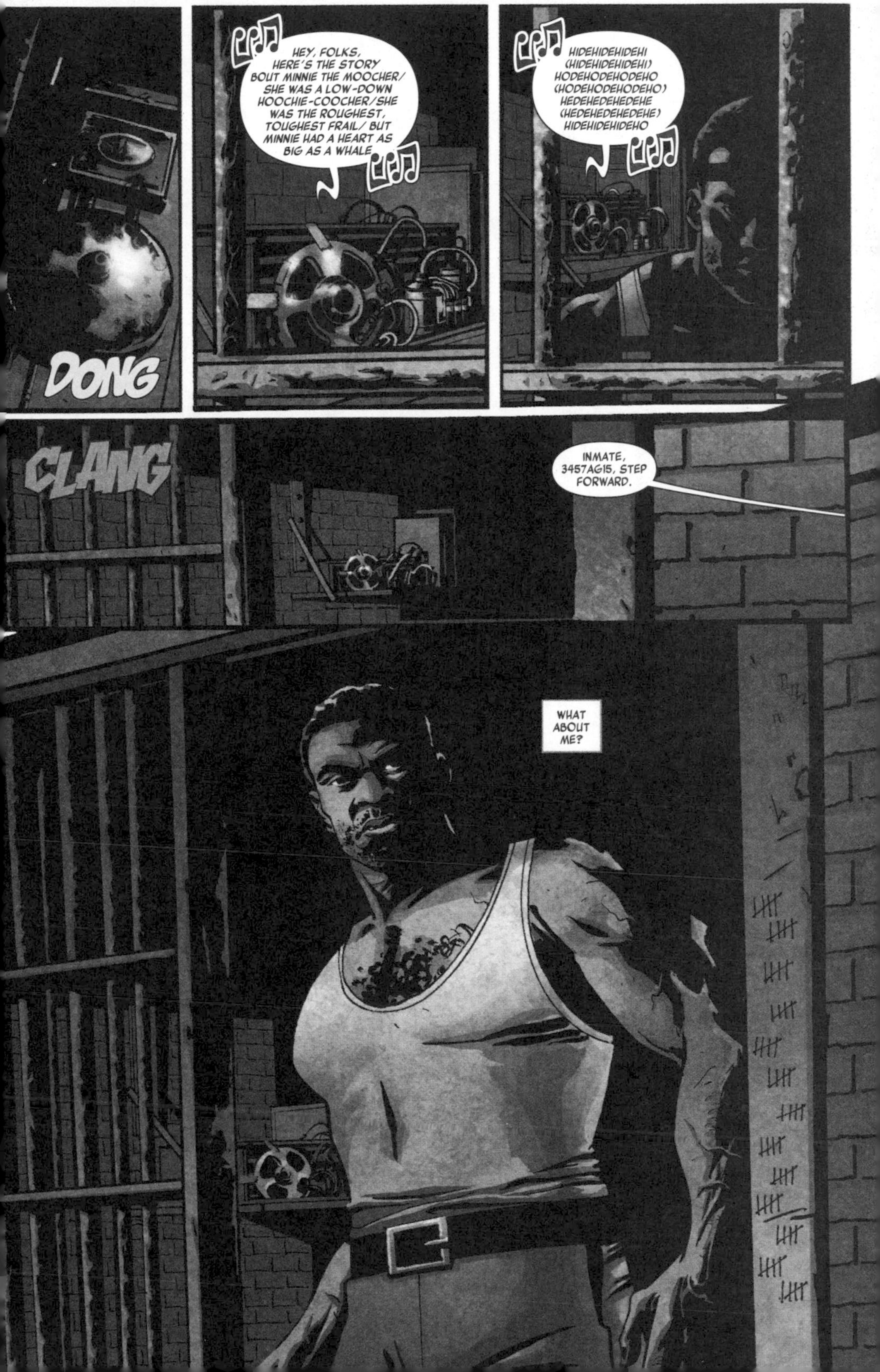
DONG
HEY, FOLKS, HERE'S THE STORY BOUT MINNIE THE MOOCHER/ SHE WAS A LOW-DOWN HOOCHIE-COOCHER/ SHE WAS THE ROUGHEST, TOUGHEST FRAIL/ BUT MINNIE HAD A HEART AS BIG AS A WHALE
HIDEHIDEHIDEHI (HIDEHIDEHIDEHI) HODEHODEHODEHO (HODEHODEHODEHO) HEDEHEDEHEDEHE (HEDEHEDEHEDEHE) HIDEHIDEHIDEHO
CLANG
INMATE, 3457AG15, STEP FORWARD.
WHAT ABOUT ME?

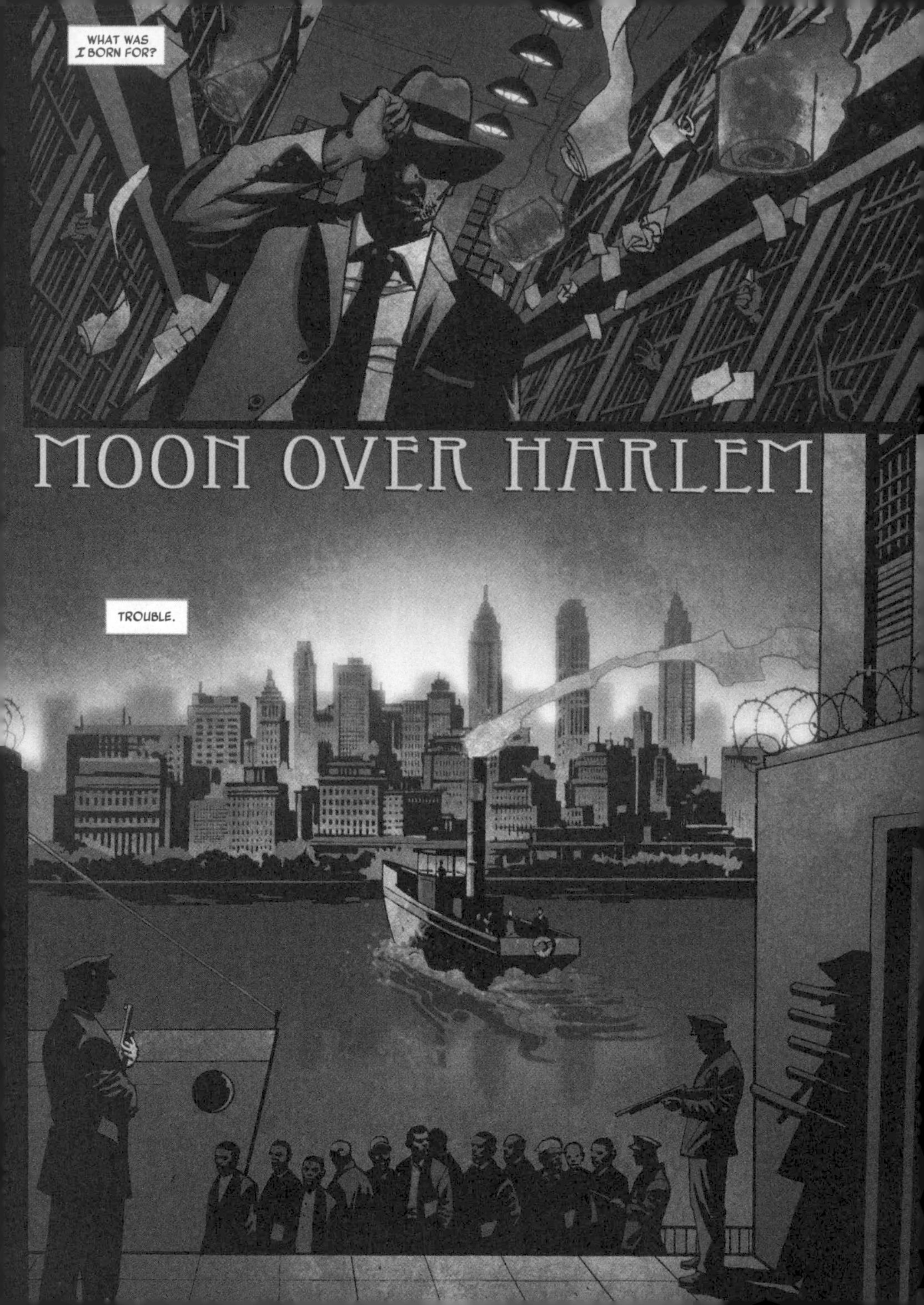
WHAT WAS I BORN FOR?
MOON OVER HARLEM
TROUBLE.

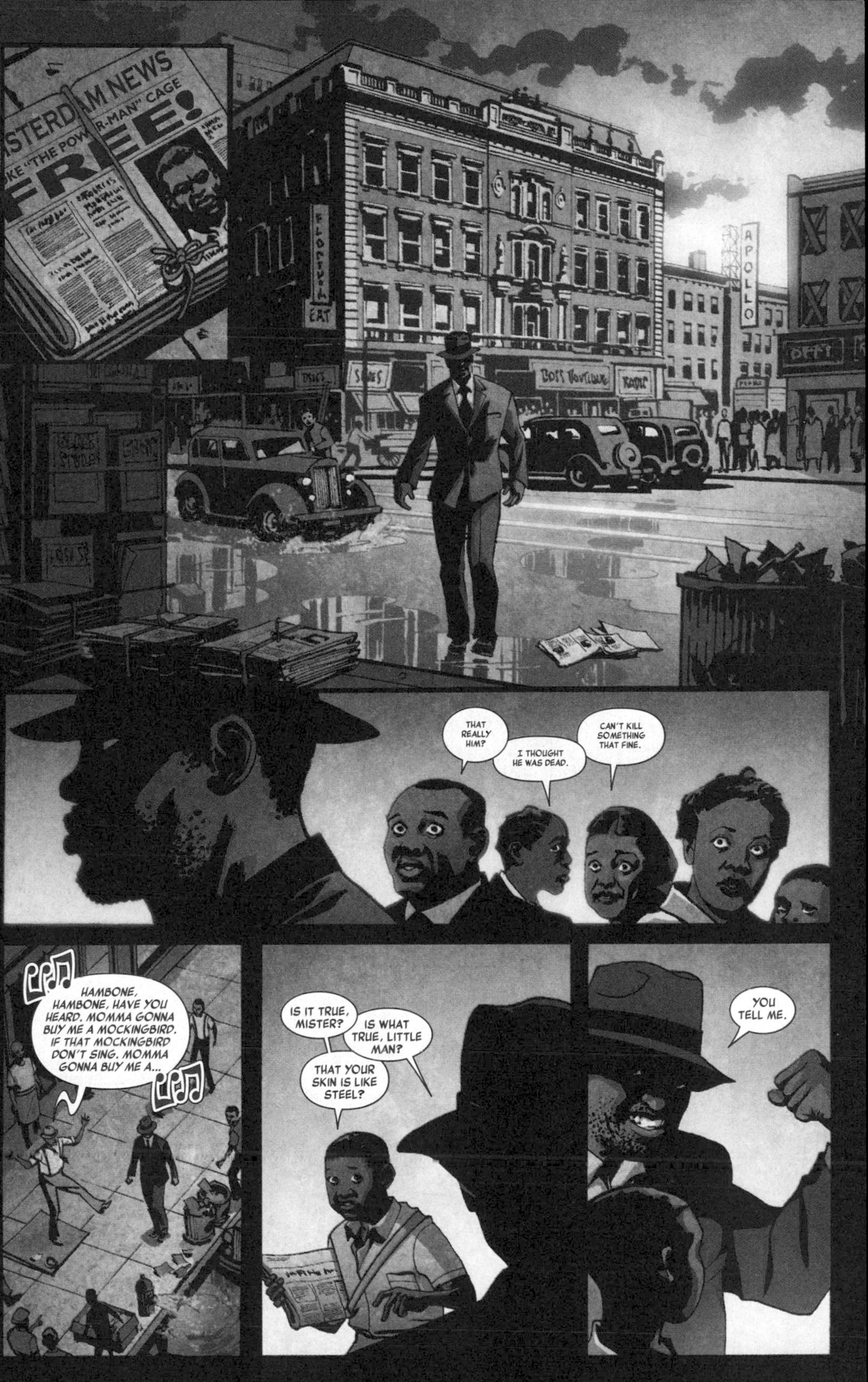
AMSTERDAM NEWS
"THE POWER-MAN" CAGE
FREE!
APOLLO
EAT
BOSS BOUTIQUE
THAT REALLY HIM?
I THOUGHT HE WAS DEAD.
CAN'T KILL SOMETHING THAT FINE.
HAMBONE, HAMBONE, HAVE YOU HEARD. MOMMA GONNA BUY ME A MOCKINGBIRD. IF THAT MOCKINGBIRD DON'T SING. MOMMA GONNA BUY ME A...
IS IT TRUE, MISTER?
IS WHAT TRUE, LITTLE MAN?
THAT YOUR SKIN IS LIKE STEEL?
YOU TELL ME.

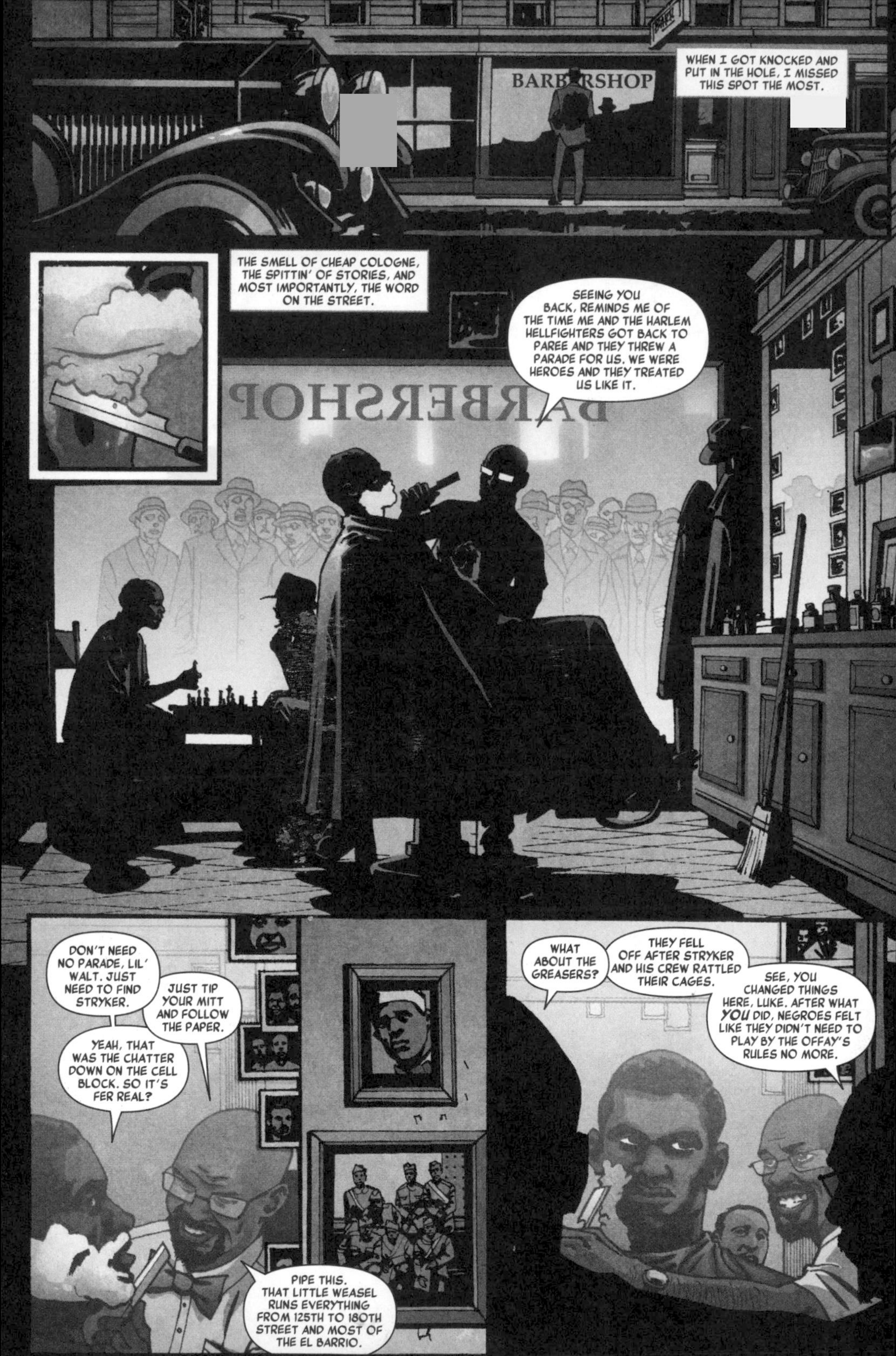
BARBERSHOP
WHEN I GOT KNOCKED AND PUT IN THE HOLE, I MISSED THIS SPOT THE MOST.
THE SMELL OF CHEAP COLOGNE, THE SPITTIN' OF STORIES, AND MOST IMPORTANTLY, THE WORD ON THE STREET.
SEEING YOU BACK, REMINDS ME OF THE TIME ME AND THE HARLEM HELLFIGHTERS GOT BACK TO PAREE AND THEY THREW A PARADE FOR US. WE WERE HEROES AND THEY TREATED US LIKE IT.
DON'T NEED NO PARADE, LIL' WALT. JUST NEED TO FIND STRYKER.
JUST TIP YOUR MITT AND FOLLOW THE PAPER.
YEAH, THAT WAS THE CHATTER DOWN ON THE CELL BLOCK. SO IT'S FER REAL?
PIPE THIS. THAT LITTLE WEASEL RUNS EVERYTHING FROM 125TH TO 180TH STREET AND MOST OF THE EL BARRIO.
WHAT ABOUT THE GREASERS?
THEY FELL OFF AFTER STRYKER AND HIS CREW RATTLED THEIR CAGES.
SEE, YOU CHANGED THINGS HERE, LUKE. AFTER WHAT *YOU* DID, NEGROES FELT LIKE THEY DIDN'T NEED TO PLAY BY THE OFFAY'S RULES NO MORE.

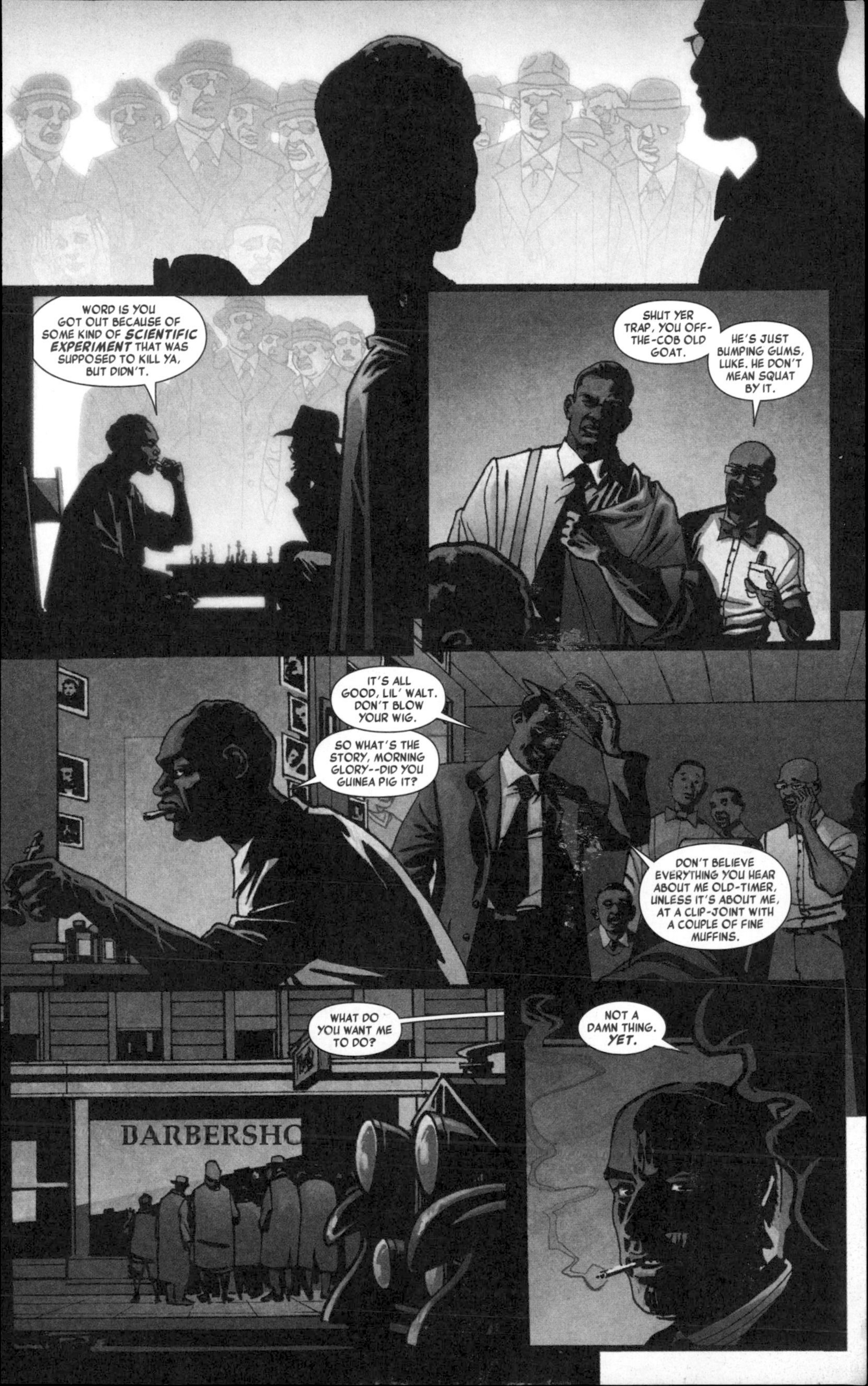
WORD IS YOU GOT OUT BECAUSE OF SOME KIND OF SCIENTIFIC EXPERIMENT THAT WAS SUPPOSED TO KILL YA, BUT DIDN'T.
SHUT YER TRAP, YOU OFF-THE-COB OLD GOAT.
HE'S JUST BUMPING GUMS, LUKE. HE DON'T MEAN SQUAT BY IT.
IT'S ALL GOOD, LIL' WALT. DON'T BLOW YOUR WIG.
SO WHAT'S THE STORY, MORNING GLORY--DID YOU GUINEA PIG IT?
DON'T BELIEVE EVERYTHING YOU HEAR ABOUT ME OLD-TIMER, UNLESS IT'S ABOUT ME, AT A CLIP-JOINT WITH A COUPLE OF FINE MUFFINS.
BARBERSHO
WHAT DO YOU WANT ME TO DO?
NOT A DAMN THING. YET.

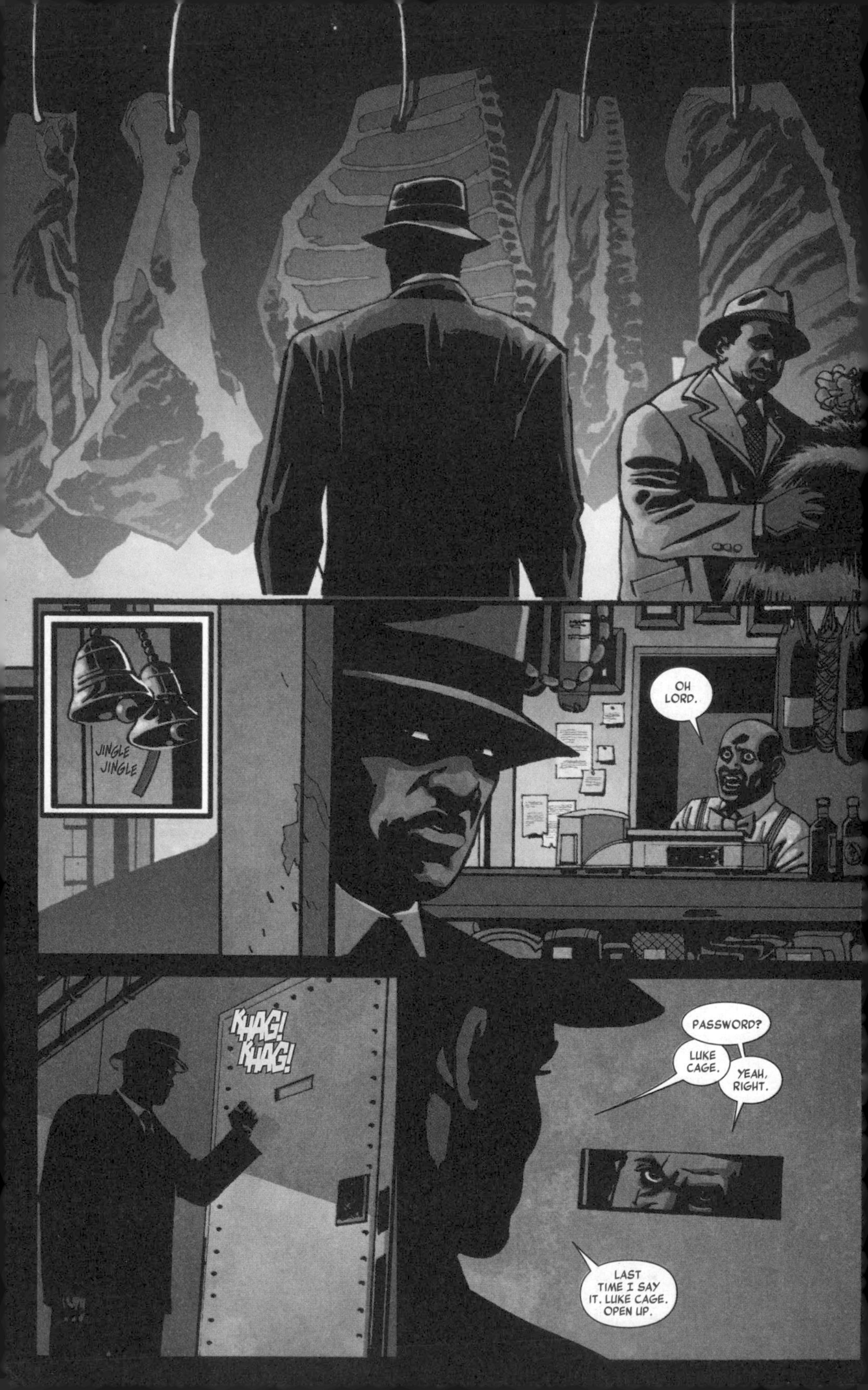
JINGLE JINGLE
OH LORD.
KHAG! KHAG!
PASSWORD?
LUKE CAGE.
YEAH, RIGHT.
LAST TIME I SAY IT. LUKE CAGE. OPEN UP.

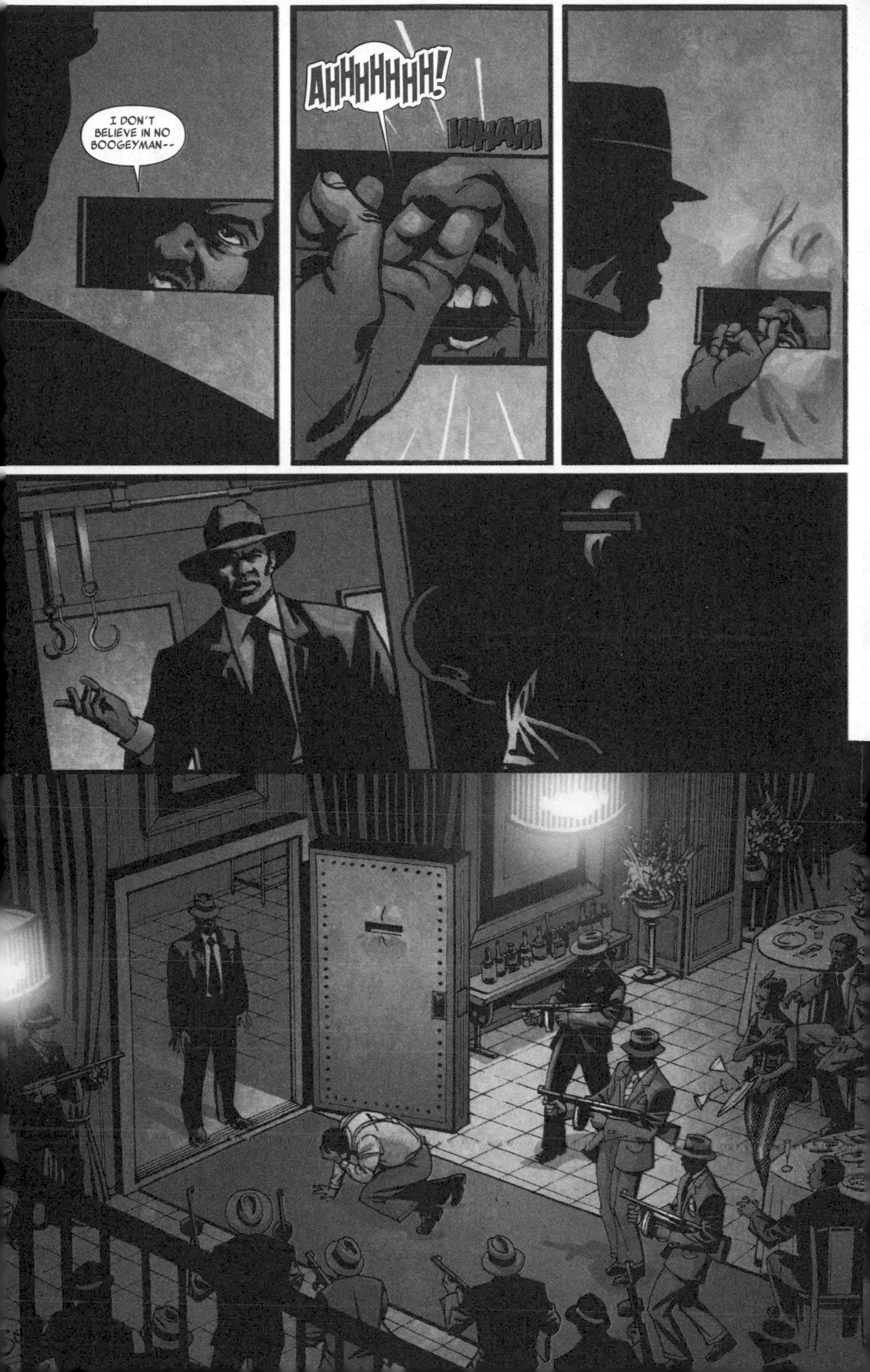
I DON'T BELIEVE IN NO BOOGEYMAN--
AHHHHHHH!
WHAM

BREAK IT UP, YOU LUGS, YOU'D BE SQUIRTING LEAD FOR NUTHIN', THIS HERE IS THE ONE AND ONLY LUKE CAGE.
THE POWER-MAN?
YEP. THAT'S HIM.
WELCOME HOME, BLACK.
GOOD TO BE BACK, STRYKER.
BUNKY, CLEAN YOURSELF UP AFTER YA GET ME AND MY BOY HERE A COUPLE STIFF ONES.
RIGHT, BOSS.

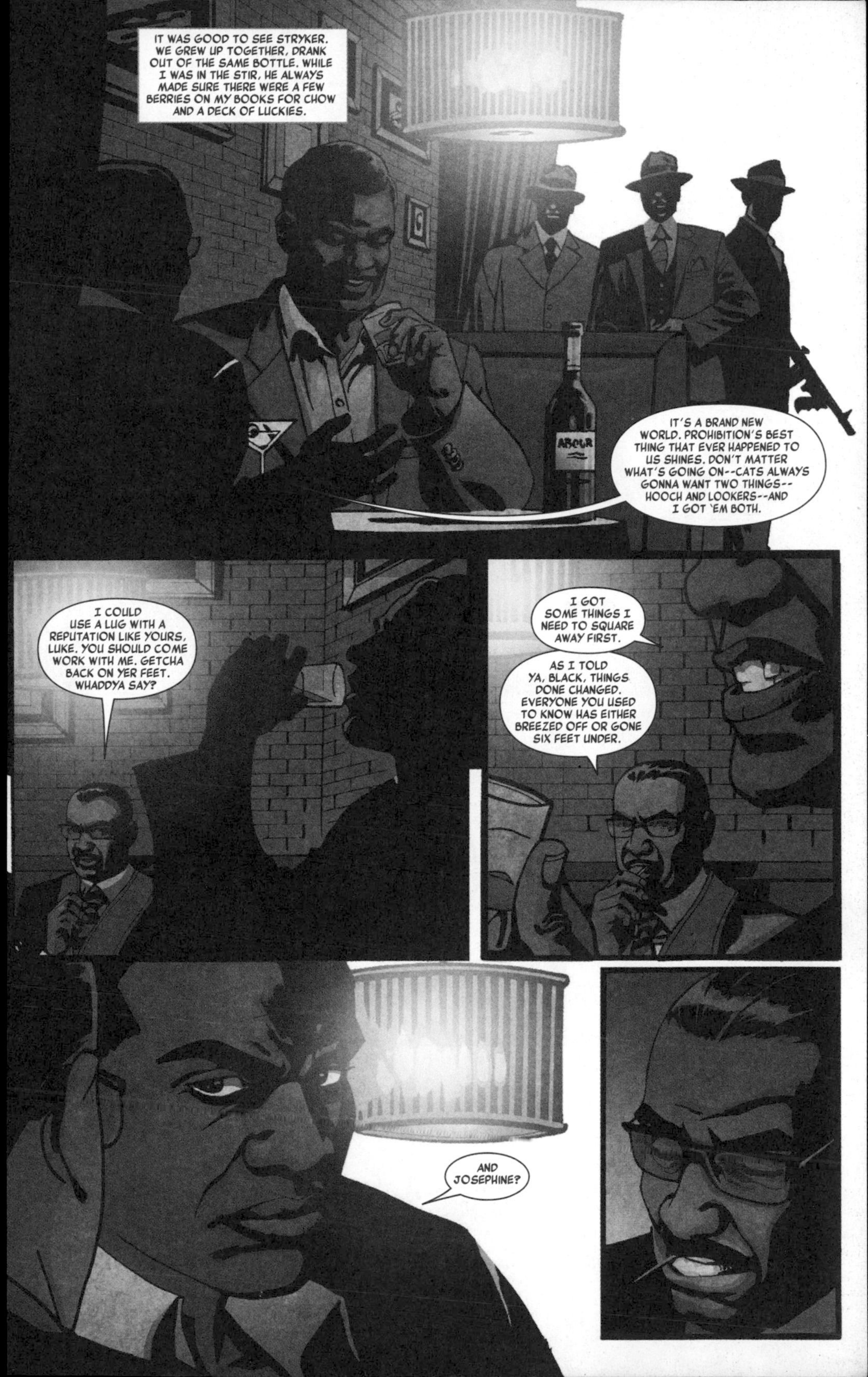
IT WAS GOOD TO SEE STRYKER. WE GREW UP TOGETHER, DRANK OUT OF THE SAME BOTTLE. WHILE I WAS IN THE STIR, HE ALWAYS MADE SURE THERE WERE A FEW BERRIES ON MY BOOKS FOR CHOW AND A DECK OF LUCKIES.
IT'S A BRAND NEW WORLD. PROHIBITION'S BEST THING THAT EVER HAPPENED TO US SHINES. DON'T MATTER WHAT'S GOING ON--CATS ALWAYS GONNA WANT TWO THINGS--HOOCH AND LOOKERS--AND I GOT 'EM BOTH.
I COULD USE A LUG WITH A REPUTATION LIKE YOURS, LUKE. YOU SHOULD COME WORK WITH ME. GETCHA BACK ON YER FEET. WHADDYA SAY?
I GOT SOME THINGS I NEED TO SQUARE AWAY FIRST.
AS I TOLD YA, BLACK, THINGS DONE CHANGED. EVERYONE YOU USED TO KNOW HAS EITHER BREEZED OFF OR GONE SIX FEET UNDER.
AND JOSEPHINE?

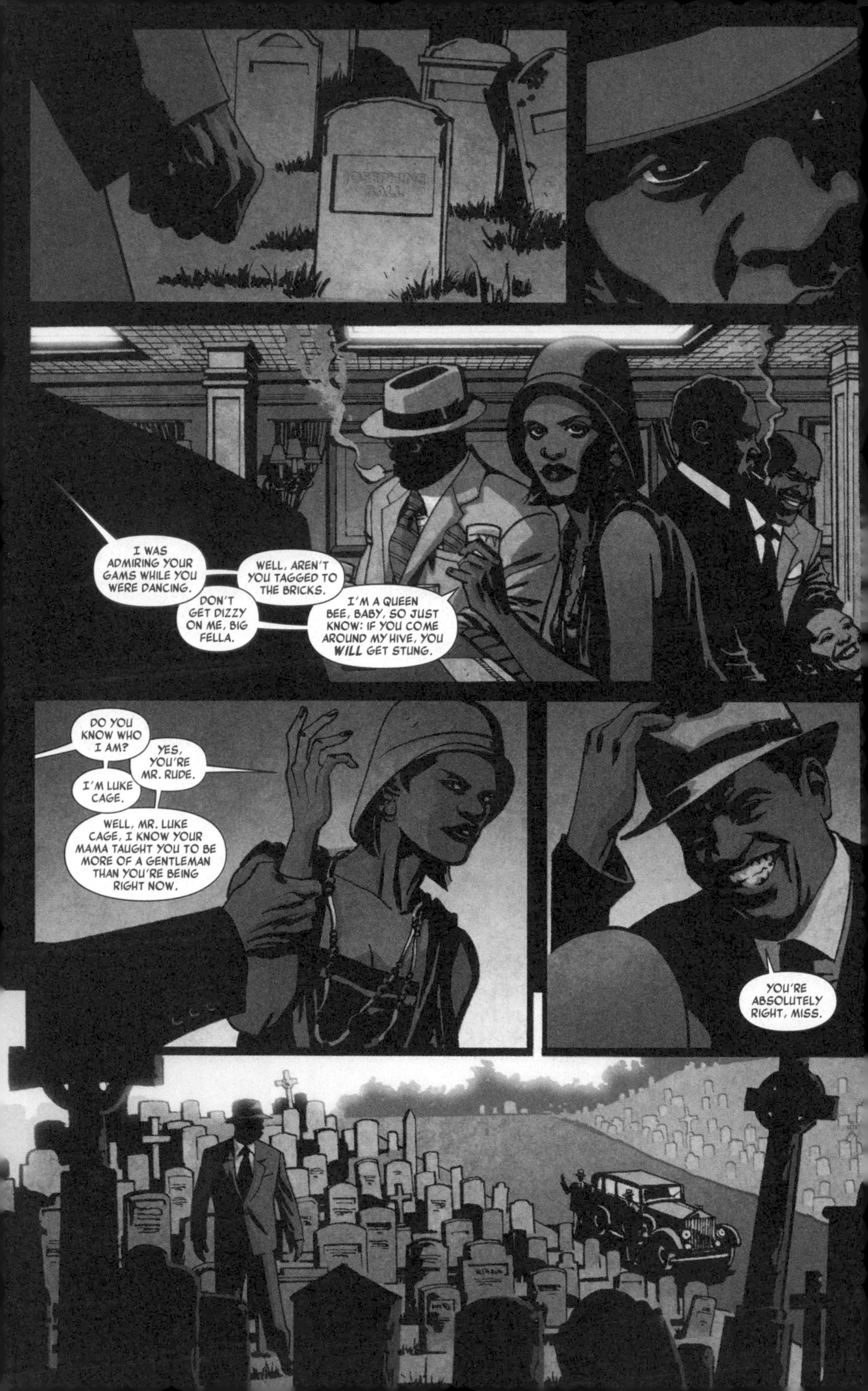
JOSEPHINE BALL
I WAS ADMIRING YOUR GAMS WHILE YOU WERE DANCING.
WELL, AREN'T YOU TAGGED TO THE BRICKS.
DON'T GET DIZZY ON ME, BIG FELLA.
I'M A QUEEN BEE, BABY, SO JUST KNOW: IF YOU COME AROUND MY HIVE, YOU **WILL** GET STUNG.
DO YOU KNOW WHO I AM?
YES, YOU'RE MR. RUDE.
I'M LUKE CAGE.
WELL, MR. LUKE CAGE, I KNOW YOUR MAMA TAUGHT YOU TO BE MORE OF A GENTLEMAN THAN YOU'RE BEING RIGHT NOW.
YOU'RE ABSOLUTELY RIGHT, MISS.

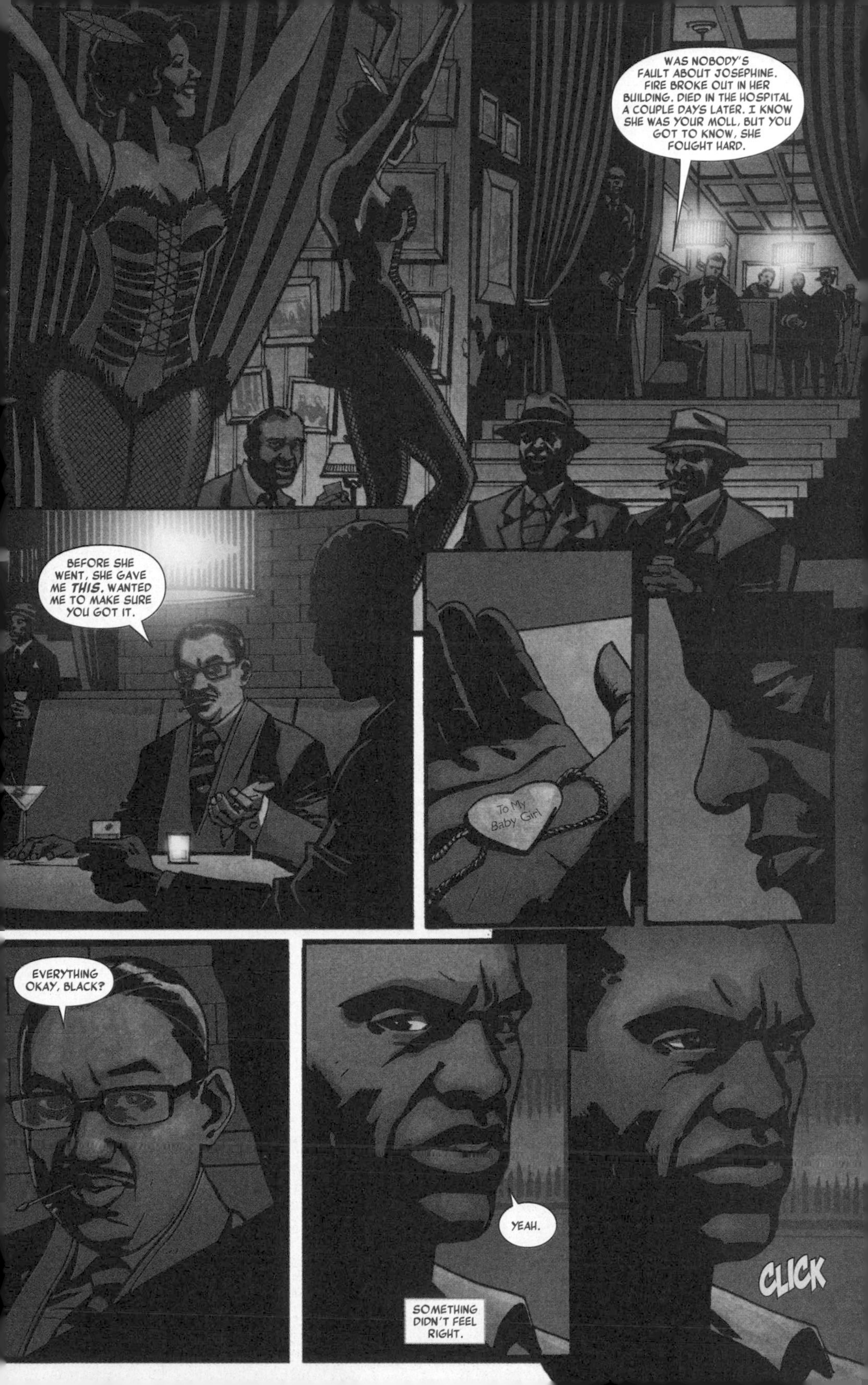
WAS NOBODY'S FAULT ABOUT JOSEPHINE. FIRE BROKE OUT IN HER BUILDING. DIED IN THE HOSPITAL A COUPLE DAYS LATER. I KNOW SHE WAS YOUR MOLL, BUT YOU GOT TO KNOW, SHE FOUGHT HARD.
BEFORE SHE WENT, SHE GAVE ME ***THIS.*** WANTED ME TO MAKE SURE YOU GOT IT.
To My Baby Girl
EVERYTHING OKAY, BLACK?
YEAH.
SOMETHING DIDN'T FEEL RIGHT.
CLICK

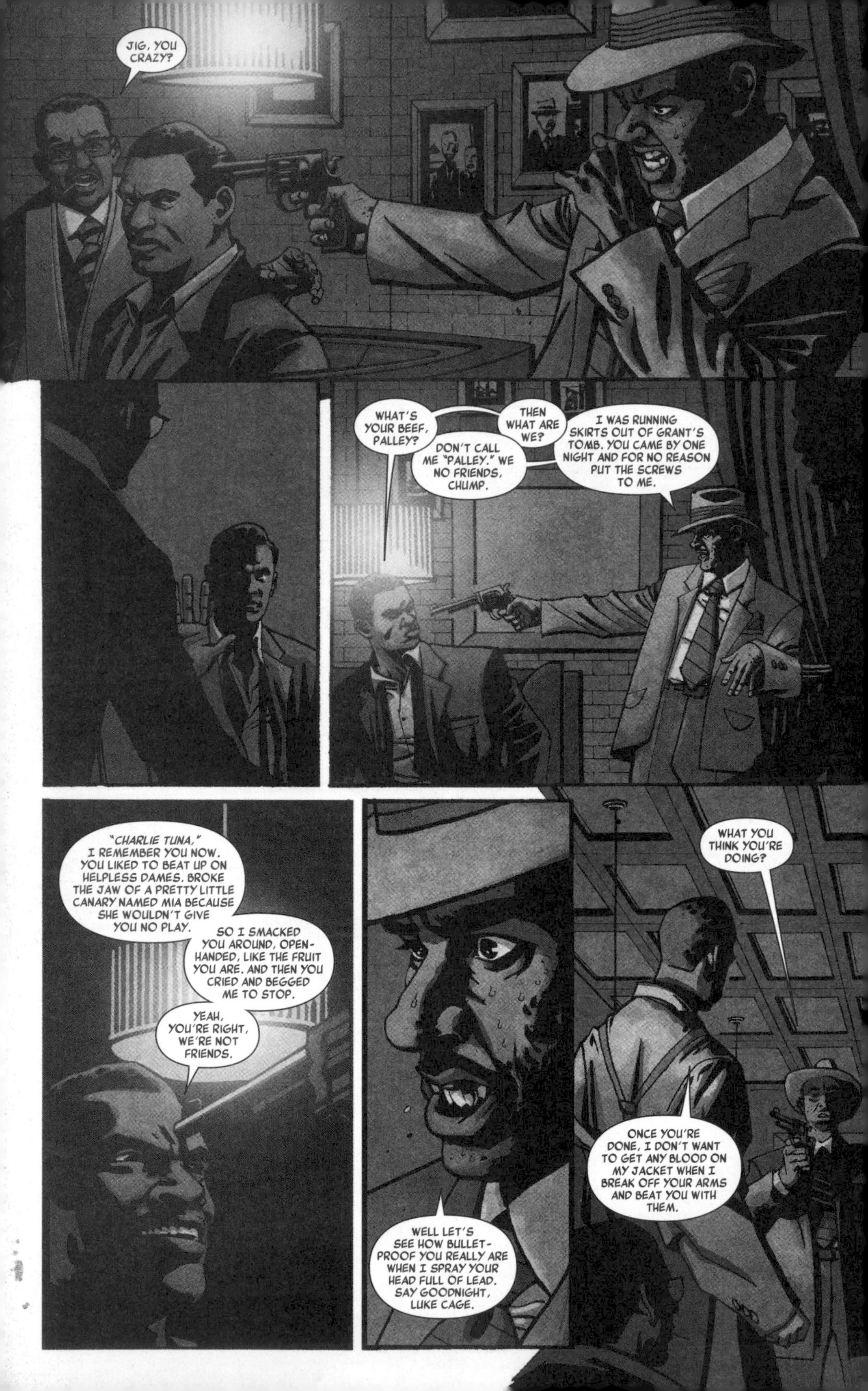

JIG, YOU CRAZY?
WHAT'S YOUR BEEF, PALLEY?
DON'T CALL ME "PALLEY." WE NO FRIENDS, CHUMP.
THEN WHAT ARE WE?
I WAS RUNNING SKIRTS OUT OF GRANT'S TOMB. YOU CAME BY ONE NIGHT AND FOR NO REASON PUT THE SCREWS TO ME.
"CHARLIE TUNA," I REMEMBER YOU NOW. YOU LIKED TO BEAT UP ON HELPLESS DAMES. BROKE THE JAW OF A PRETTY LITTLE CANARY NAMED MIA BECAUSE SHE WOULDN'T GIVE YOU NO PLAY.
SO I SMACKED YOU AROUND, OPEN-HANDED, LIKE THE FRUIT YOU ARE. AND THEN YOU CRIED AND BEGGED ME TO STOP.
YEAH, YOU'RE RIGHT, WE'RE NOT FRIENDS.
WELL LET'S SEE HOW BULLET-PROOF YOU REALLY ARE WHEN I SPRAY YOUR HEAD FULL OF LEAD. SAY GOODNIGHT, LUKE CAGE.
WHAT YOU THINK YOU'RE DOING?
ONCE YOU'RE DONE, I DON'T WANT TO GET ANY BLOOD ON MY JACKET WHEN I BREAK OFF YOUR ARMS AND BEAT YOU WITH THEM.

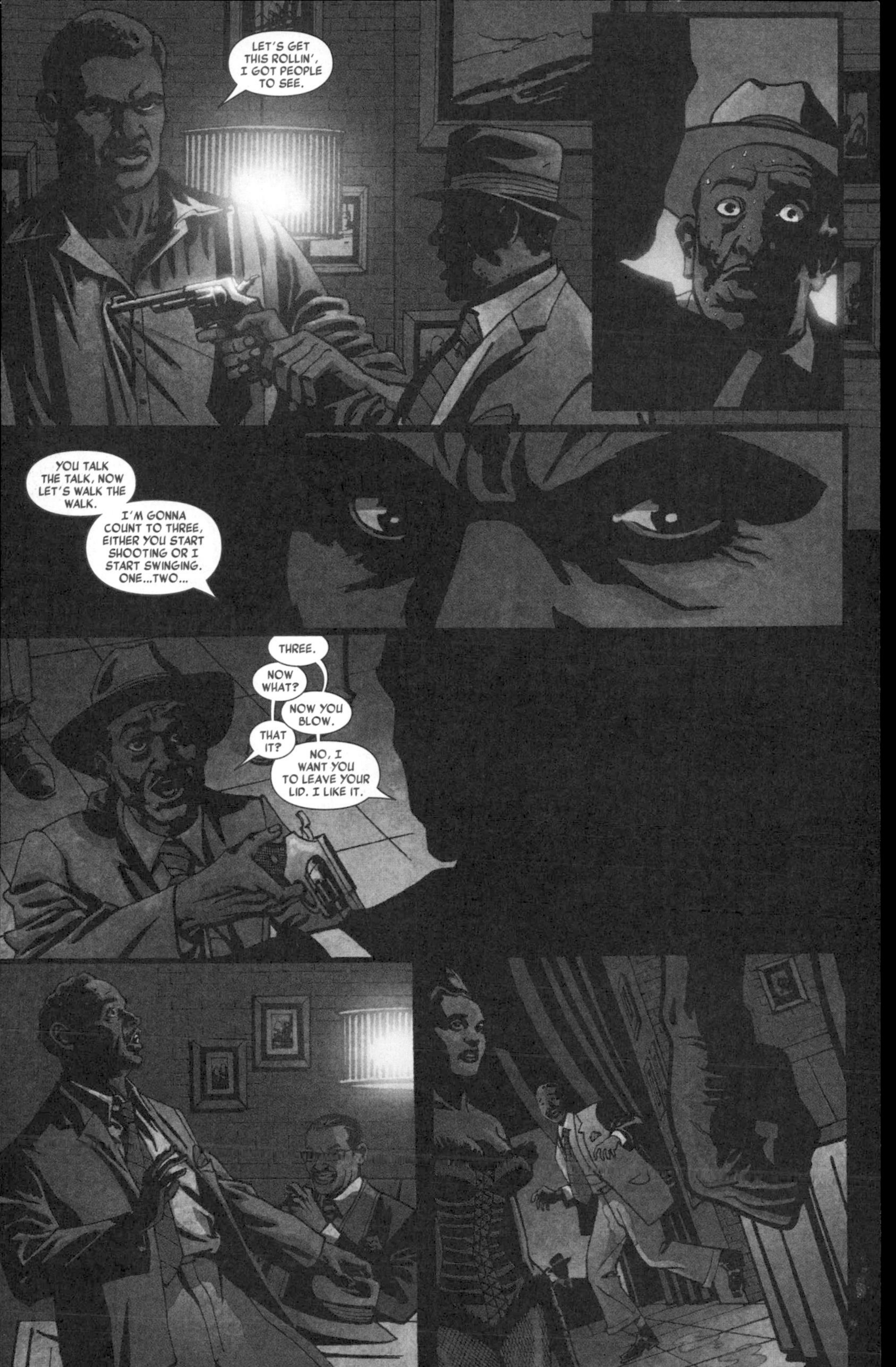
LET'S GET THIS ROLLIN', I GOT PEOPLE TO SEE.
YOU TALK THE TALK, NOW LET'S WALK THE WALK.
I'M GONNA COUNT TO THREE, EITHER YOU START SHOOTING OR I START SWINGING. ONE...TWO...
THREE.
NOW WHAT?
NOW YOU BLOW.
THAT IT?
NO, I WANT YOU TO LEAVE YOUR LID. I LIKE IT.

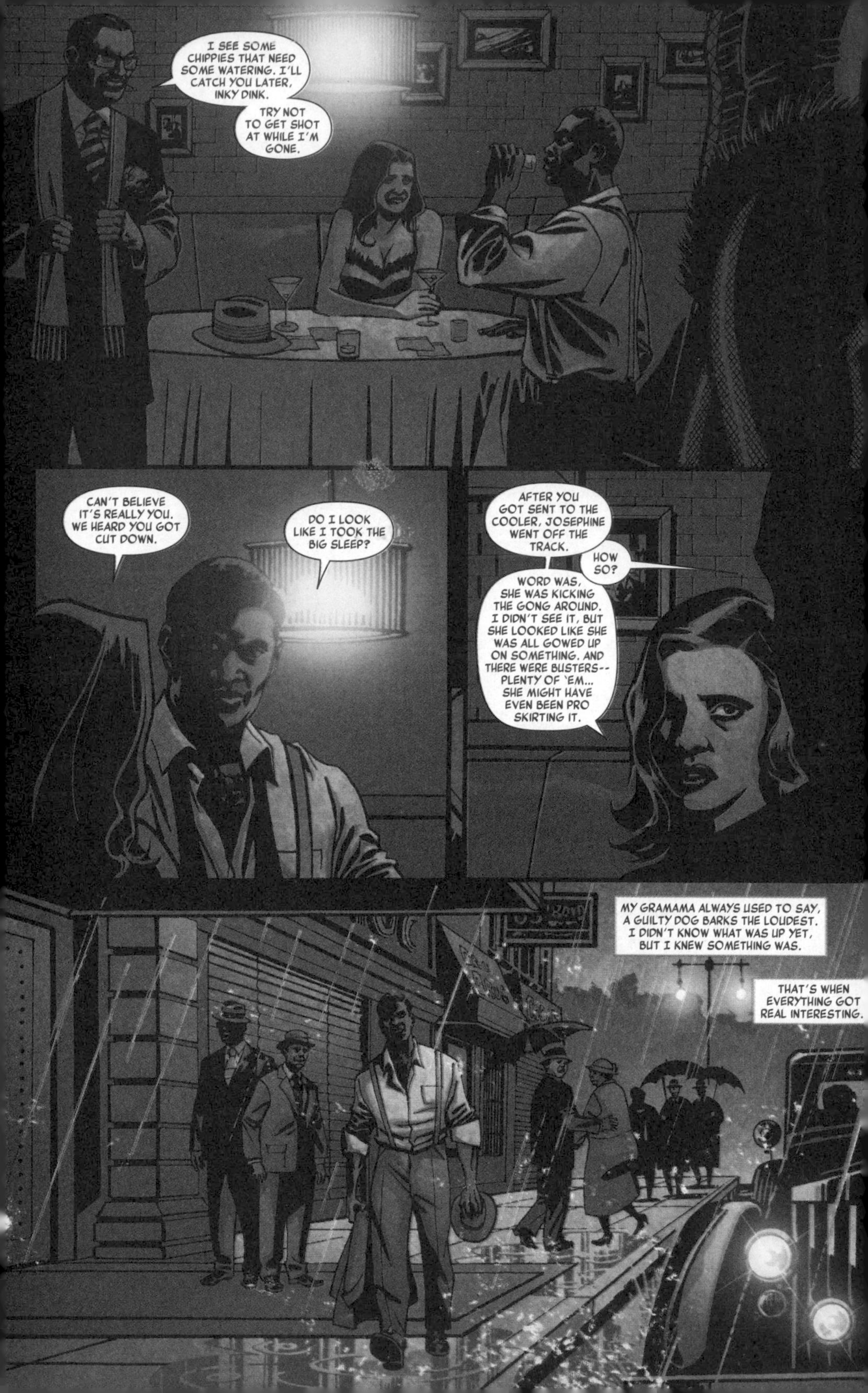
I SEE SOME CHIPPIES THAT NEED SOME WATERING. I'LL CATCH YOU LATER, INKY DINK.
TRY NOT TO GET SHOT AT WHILE I'M GONE.
CAN'T BELIEVE IT'S REALLY YOU. WE HEARD YOU GOT CUT DOWN.
DO I LOOK LIKE I TOOK THE BIG SLEEP?
AFTER YOU GOT SENT TO THE COOLER, JOSEPHINE WENT OFF THE TRACK.
HOW SO?
WORD WAS, SHE WAS KICKING THE GONG AROUND. I DIDN'T SEE IT, BUT SHE LOOKED LIKE SHE WAS ALL GOWED UP ON SOMETHING. AND THERE WERE BUSTERS-- PLENTY OF 'EM... SHE MIGHT HAVE EVEN BEEN PRO SKIRTING IT.
MY GRAMAMA ALWAYS USED TO SAY, A GUILTY DOG BARKS THE LOUDEST. I DIDN'T KNOW WHAT WAS UP YET, BUT I KNEW SOMETHING WAS.
THAT'S WHEN EVERYTHING GOT REAL INTERESTING.

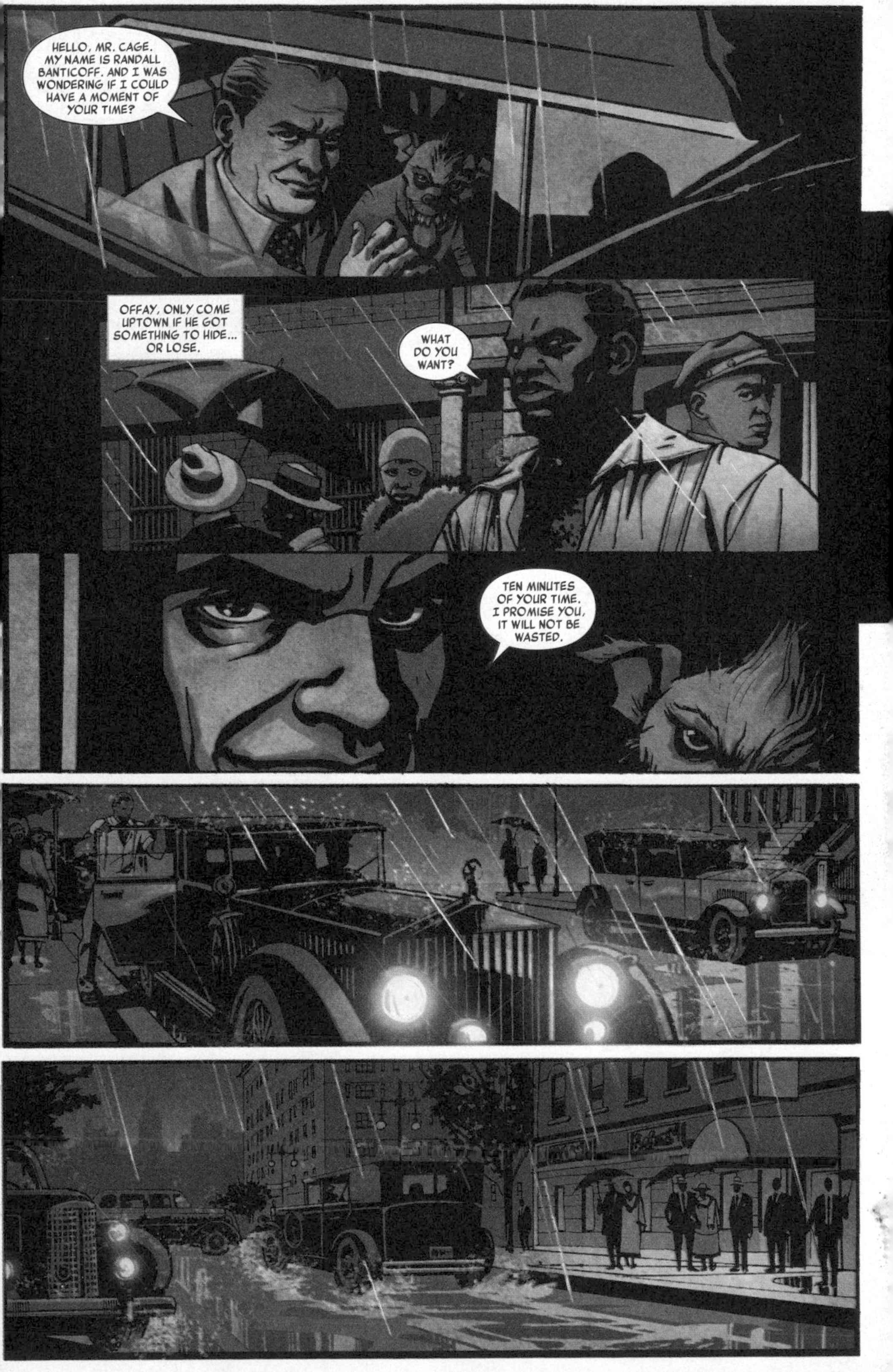
HELLO, MR. CAGE. MY NAME IS RANDALL BANTICOFF. AND I WAS WONDERING IF I COULD HAVE A MOMENT OF YOUR TIME?
OFFAY, ONLY COME UPTOWN IF HE GOT SOMETHING TO HIDE... OR LOSE.
WHAT DO YOU WANT?
TEN MINUTES OF YOUR TIME. I PROMISE YOU, IT WILL NOT BE WASTED.

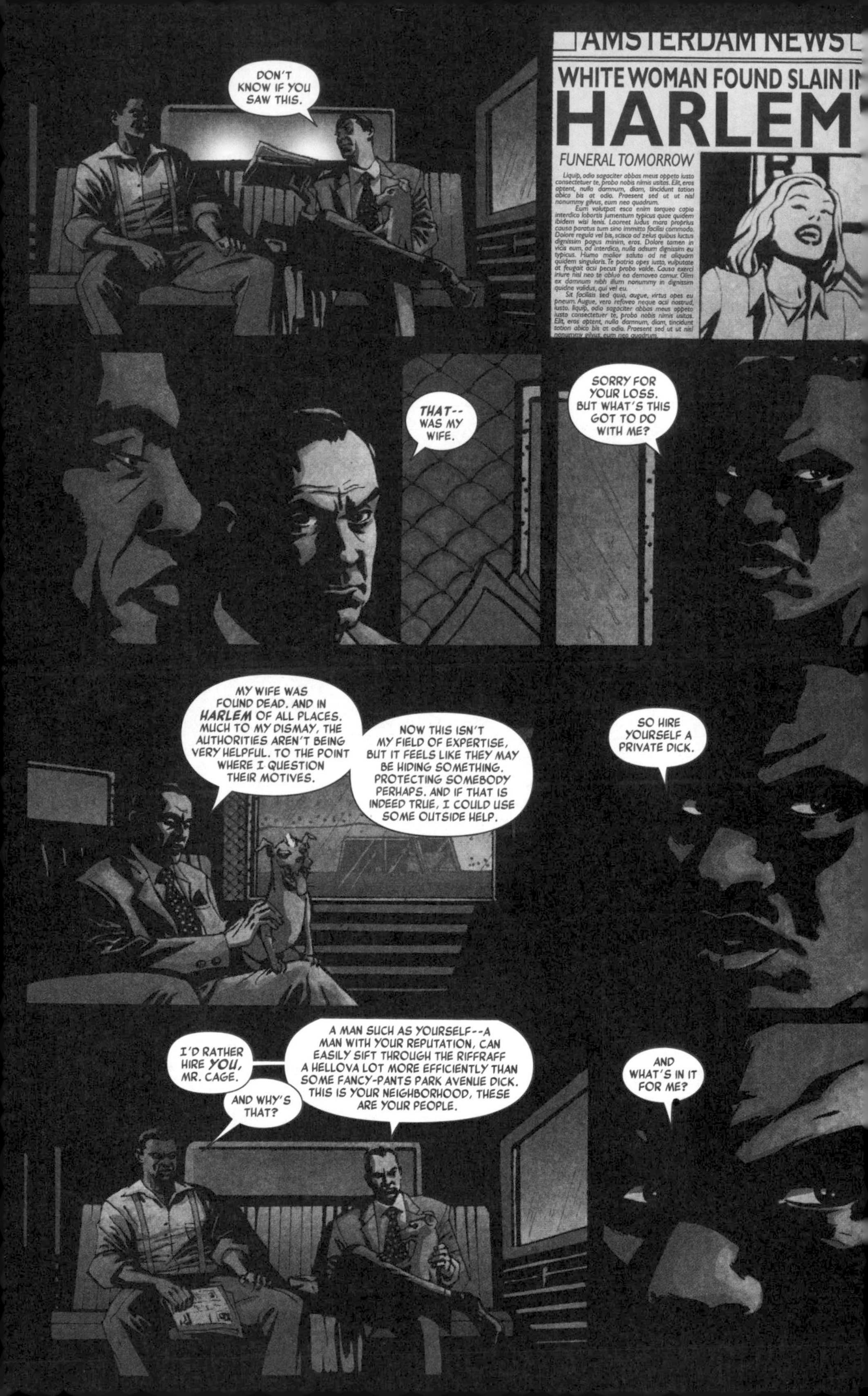

DON'T KNOW IF YOU SAW THIS.
AMSTERDAM NEWS
WHITE WOMAN FOUND SLAIN I
HARLEM
FUNERAL TOMORROW
THAT-- WAS MY WIFE.
SORRY FOR YOUR LOSS. BUT WHAT'S THIS GOT TO DO WITH ME?
MY WIFE WAS FOUND DEAD. AND IN HARLEM OF ALL PLACES. MUCH TO MY DISMAY, THE AUTHORITIES AREN'T BEING VERY HELPFUL. TO THE POINT WHERE I QUESTION THEIR MOTIVES.
NOW THIS ISN'T MY FIELD OF EXPERTISE, BUT IT FEELS LIKE THEY MAY BE HIDING SOMETHING. PROTECTING SOMEBODY PERHAPS. AND IF THAT IS INDEED TRUE, I COULD USE SOME OUTSIDE HELP.
SO HIRE YOURSELF A PRIVATE DICK.
I'D RATHER HIRE YOU, MR. CAGE.
AND WHY'S THAT?
A MAN SUCH AS YOURSELF--A MAN WITH YOUR REPUTATION, CAN EASILY SIFT THROUGH THE RIFFRAFF A HELLOVA LOT MORE EFFICIENTLY THAN SOME FANCY-PANTS PARK AVENUE DICK. THIS IS YOUR NEIGHBORHOOD, THESE ARE YOUR PEOPLE.
AND WHAT'S IN IT FOR ME?

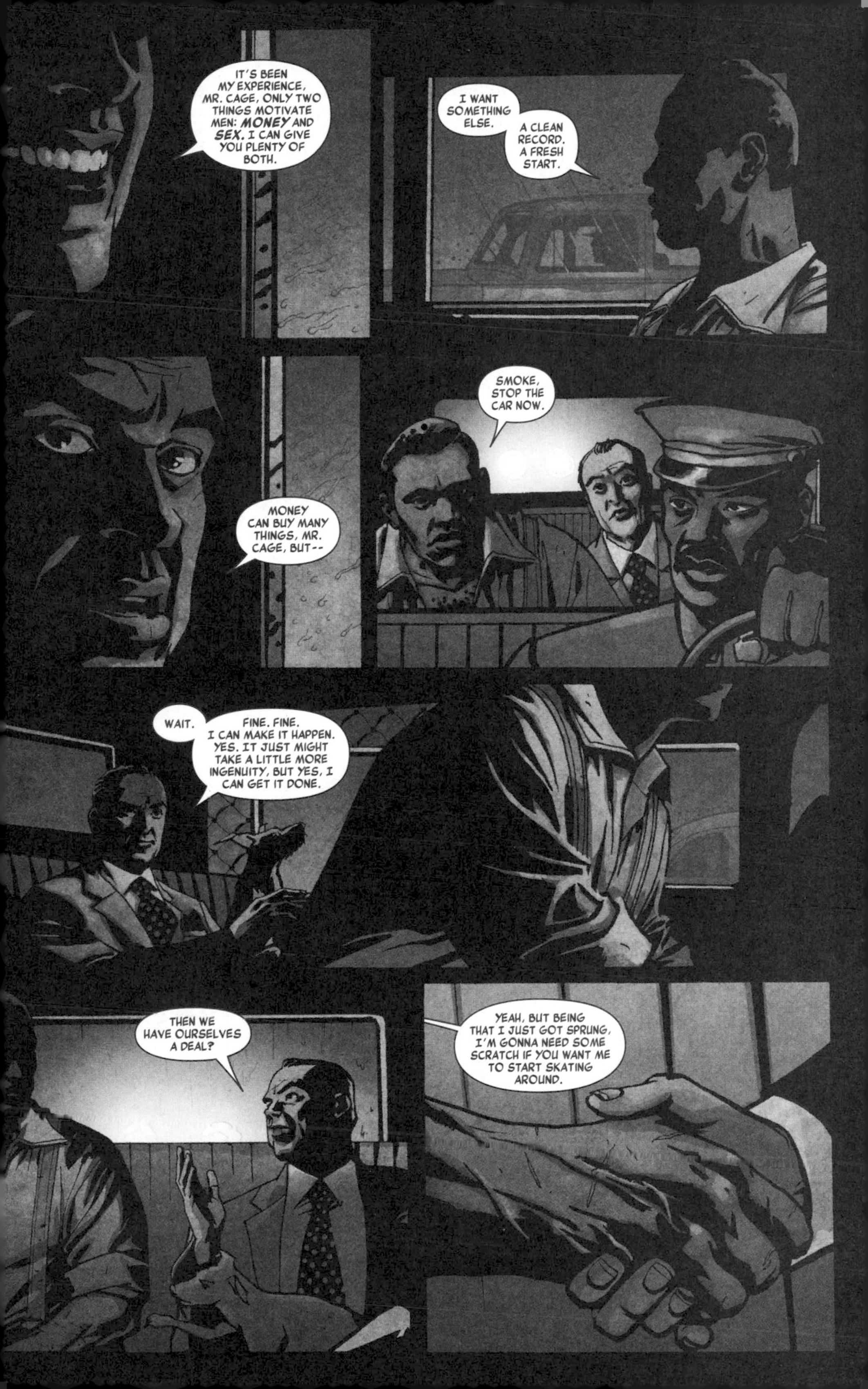

IT'S BEEN MY EXPERIENCE, MR. CAGE, ONLY TWO THINGS MOTIVATE MEN: **MONEY** AND **SEX.** I CAN GIVE YOU PLENTY OF BOTH.
I WANT SOMETHING ELSE.
A CLEAN RECORD. A FRESH START.
MONEY CAN BUY MANY THINGS, MR. CAGE, BUT--
SMOKE, STOP THE CAR NOW.
WAIT.
FINE. FINE. I CAN MAKE IT HAPPEN. YES. IT JUST MIGHT TAKE A LITTLE MORE INGENUITY, BUT YES, I CAN GET IT DONE.
THEN WE HAVE OURSELVES A DEAL?
YEAH, BUT BEING THAT I JUST GOT SPRUNG, I'M GONNA NEED SOME SCRATCH IF YOU WANT ME TO START SKATING AROUND.

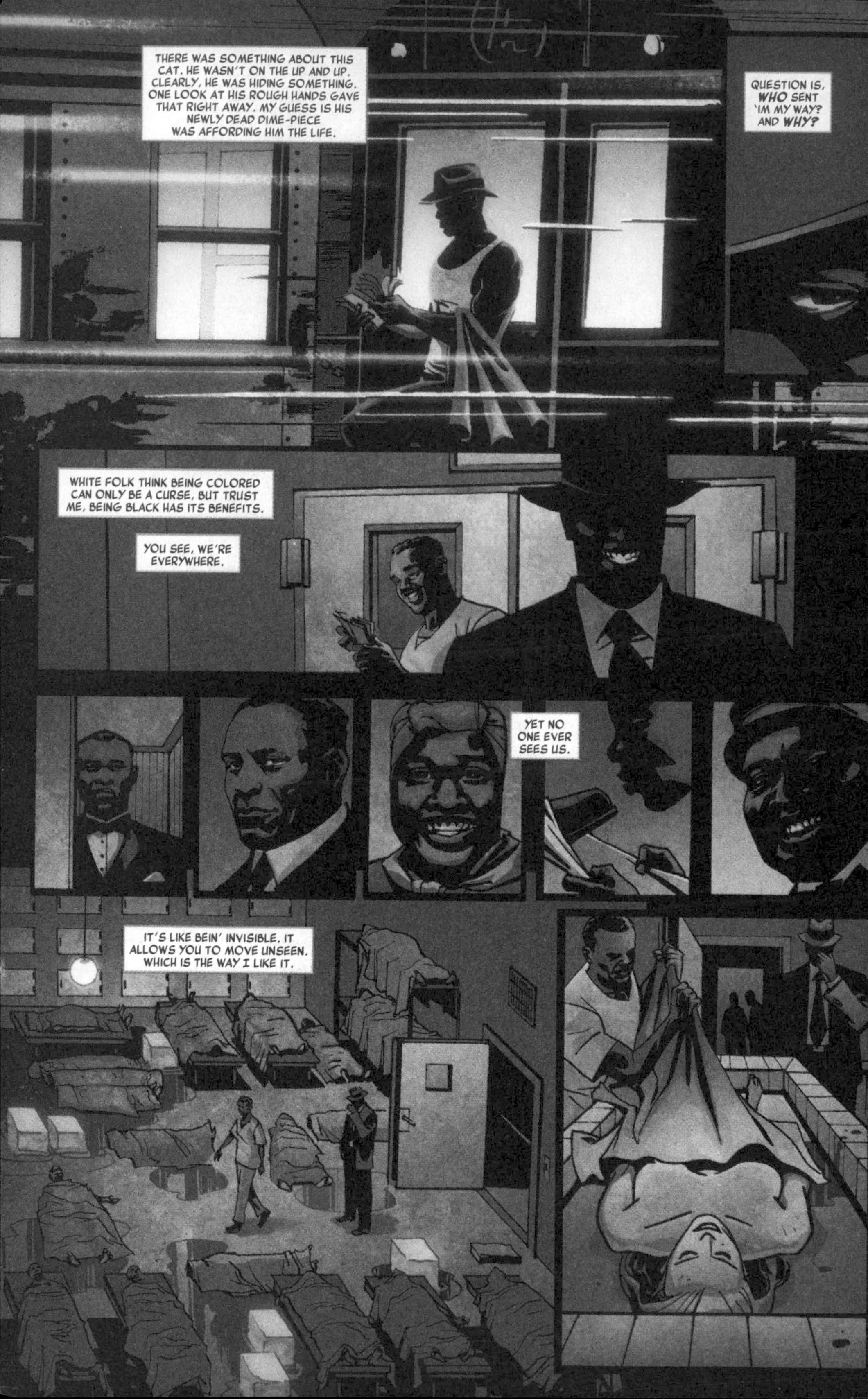
THERE WAS SOMETHING ABOUT THIS CAT. HE WASN'T ON THE UP AND UP. CLEARLY, HE WAS HIDING SOMETHING. ONE LOOK AT HIS ROUGH HANDS GAVE THAT RIGHT AWAY. MY GUESS IS HIS NEWLY DEAD DIME-PIECE WAS AFFORDING HIM THE LIFE.
QUESTION IS, WHO SENT 'IM MY WAY? AND WHY?
WHITE FOLK THINK BEING COLORED CAN ONLY BE A CURSE, BUT TRUST ME, BEING BLACK HAS ITS BENEFITS.
YOU SEE, WE'RE EVERYWHERE.
YET NO ONE EVER SEES US.
IT'S LIKE BEIN' INVISIBLE. IT ALLOWS YOU TO MOVE UNSEEN. WHICH IS THE WAY I LIKE IT.

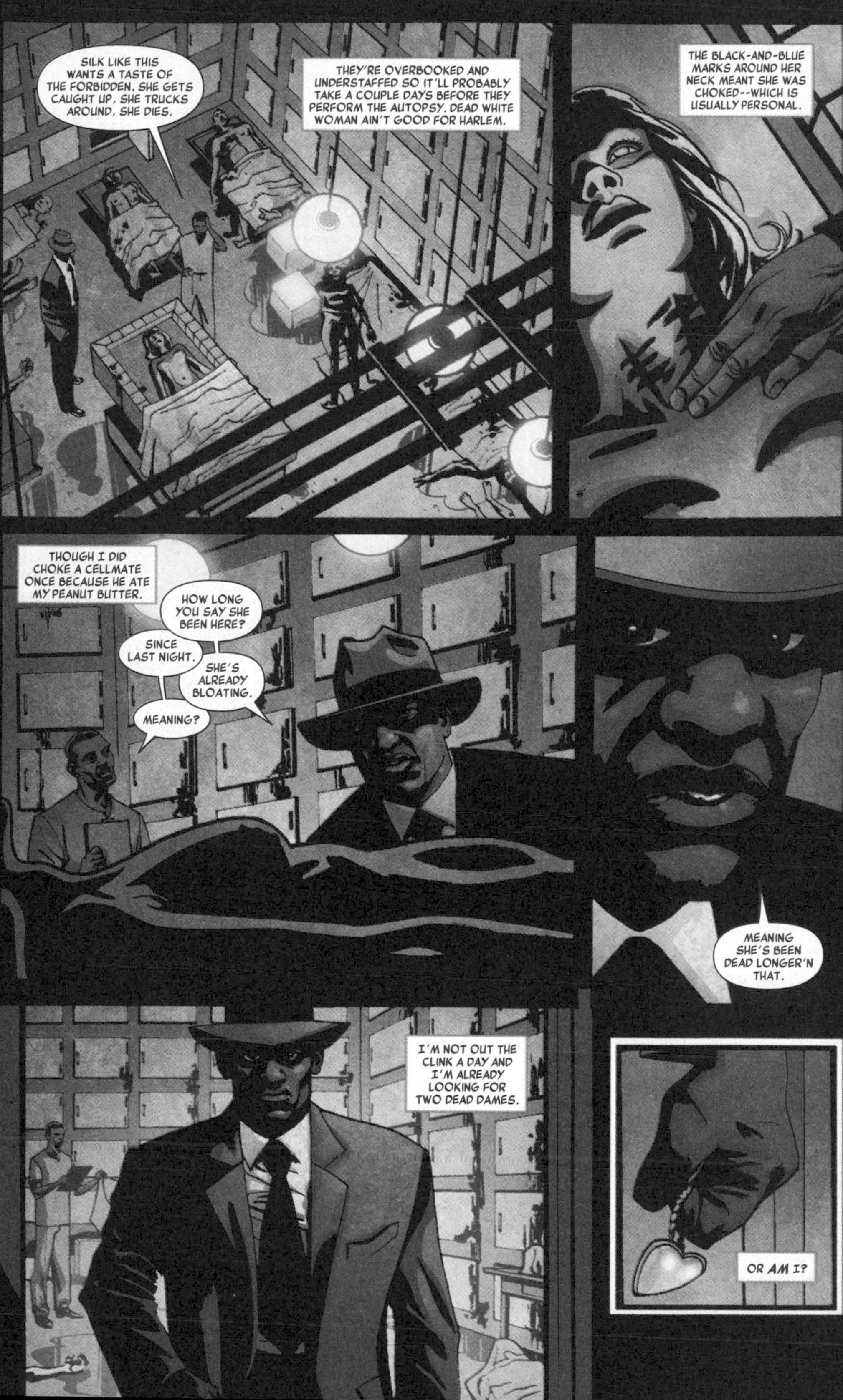
SILK LIKE THIS WANTS A TASTE OF THE FORBIDDEN. SHE GETS CAUGHT UP, SHE TRUCKS AROUND, SHE DIES.
THEY'RE OVERBOOKED AND UNDERSTAFFED SO IT'LL PROBABLY TAKE A COUPLE DAYS BEFORE THEY PERFORM THE AUTOPSY. DEAD WHITE WOMAN AIN'T GOOD FOR HARLEM.
THE BLACK-AND-BLUE MARKS AROUND HER NECK MEANT SHE WAS CHOKED--WHICH IS USUALLY PERSONAL.
THOUGH I DID CHOKE A CELLMATE ONCE BECAUSE HE ATE MY PEANUT BUTTER.
HOW LONG YOU SAY SHE BEEN HERE?
SINCE LAST NIGHT.
SHE'S ALREADY BLOATING.
MEANING?
MEANING SHE'S BEEN DEAD LONGER'N THAT.
I'M NOT OUT THE CLINK A DAY AND I'M ALREADY LOOKING FOR TWO DEAD DAMES.
OR AM I?

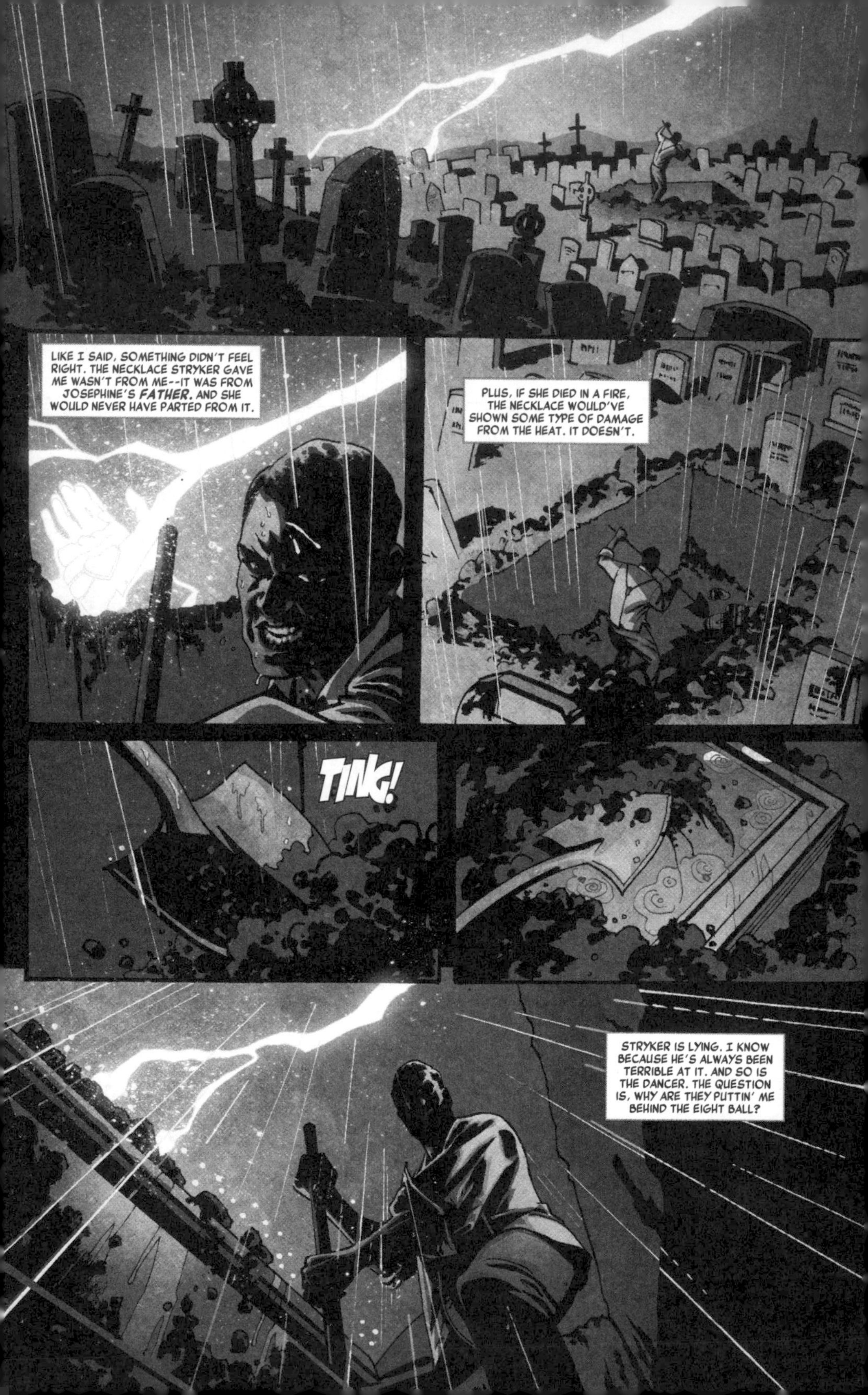
LIKE I SAID, SOMETHING DIDN'T FEEL RIGHT. THE NECKLACE STRYKER GAVE ME WASN'T FROM ME--IT WAS FROM JOSEPHINE'S FATHER. AND SHE WOULD NEVER HAVE PARTED FROM IT.
PLUS, IF SHE DIED IN A FIRE, THE NECKLACE WOULD'VE SHOWN SOME TYPE OF DAMAGE FROM THE HEAT. IT DOESN'T.
TING!
STRYKER IS LYING. I KNOW BECAUSE HE'S ALWAYS BEEN TERRIBLE AT IT. AND SO IS THE DANCER. THE QUESTION IS, WHY ARE THEY PUTTIN' ME BEHIND THE EIGHT BALL?

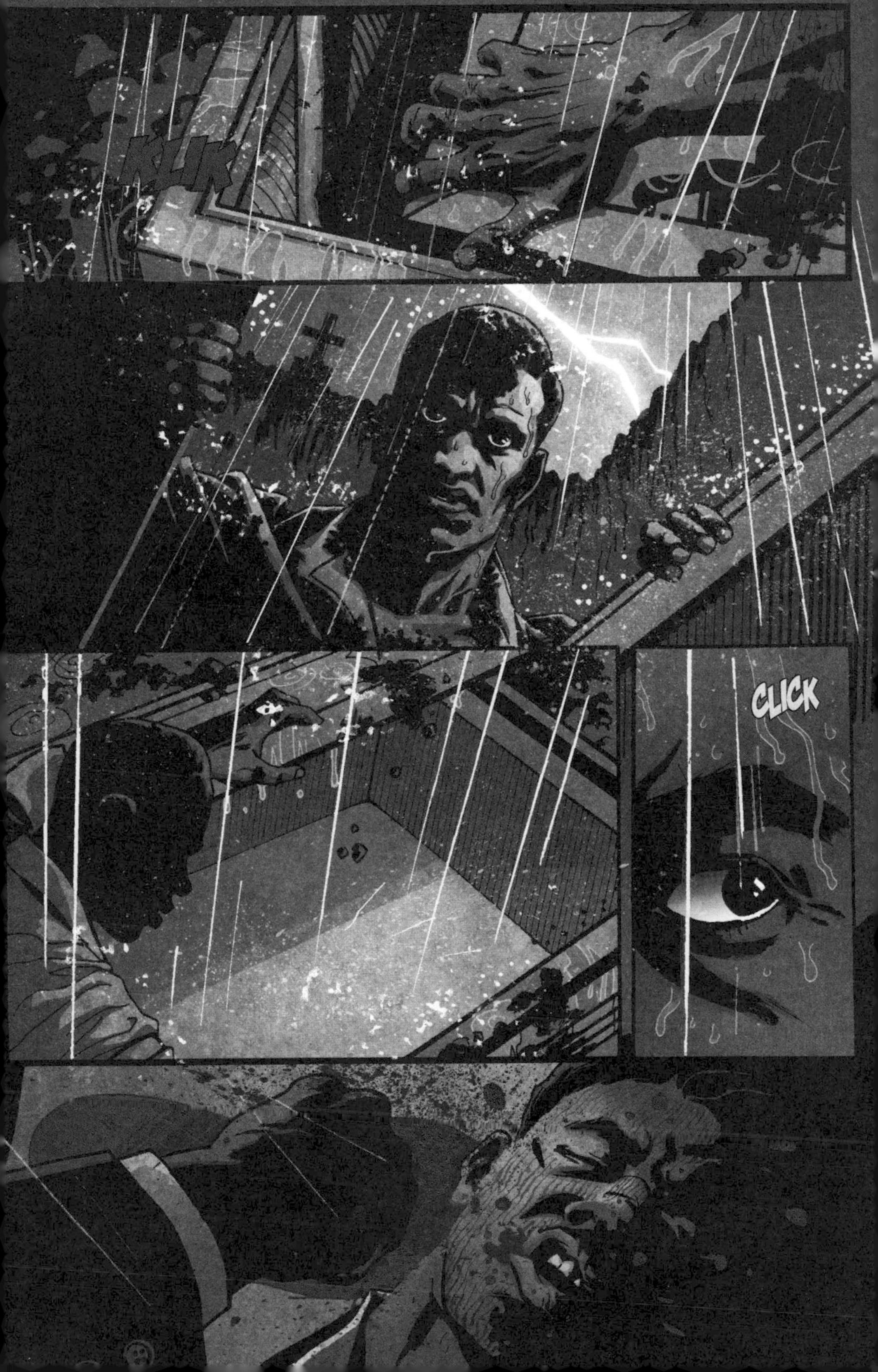
KLIK
CLICK

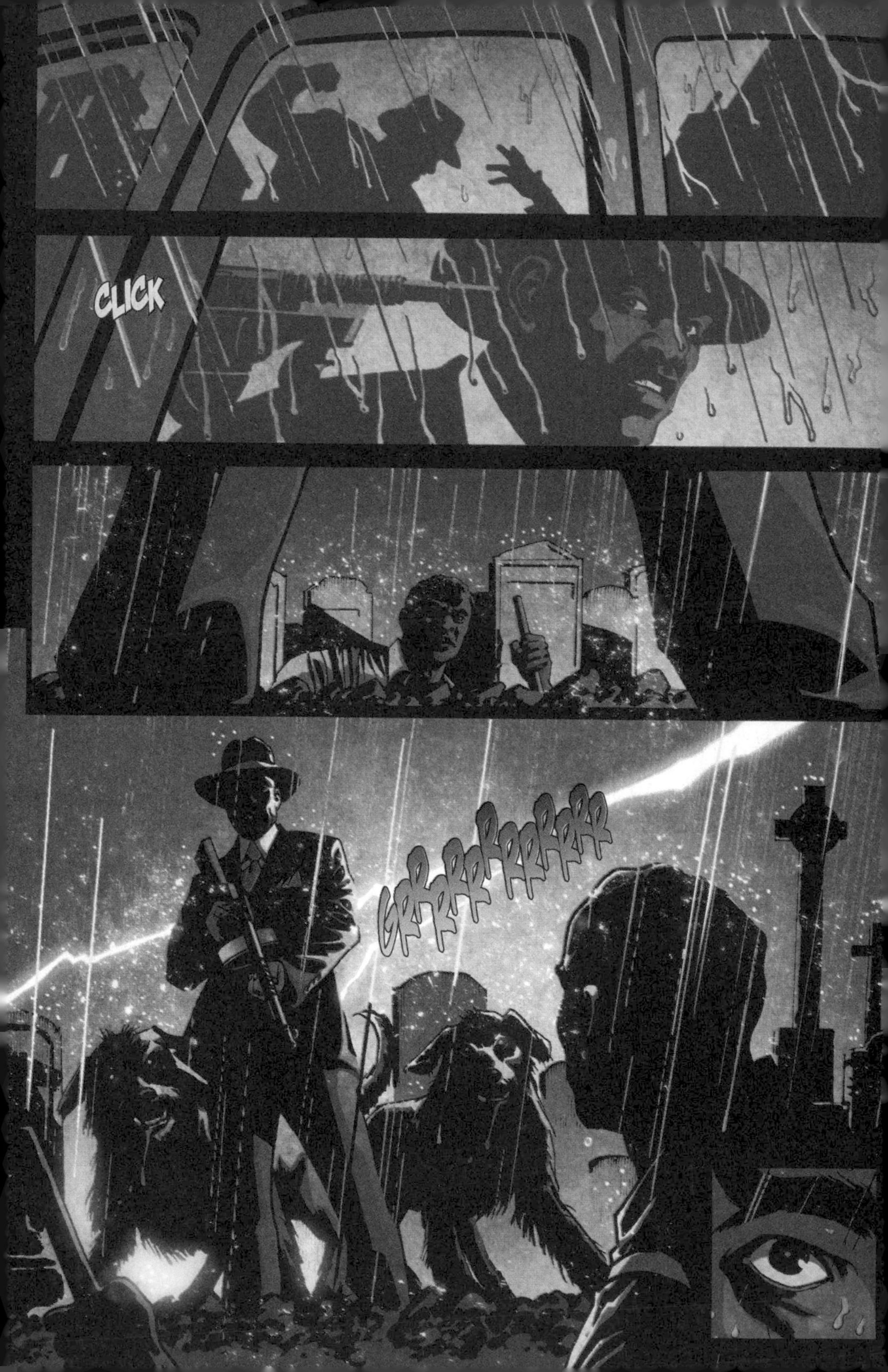
CLICK
GRRRRRRRRRR

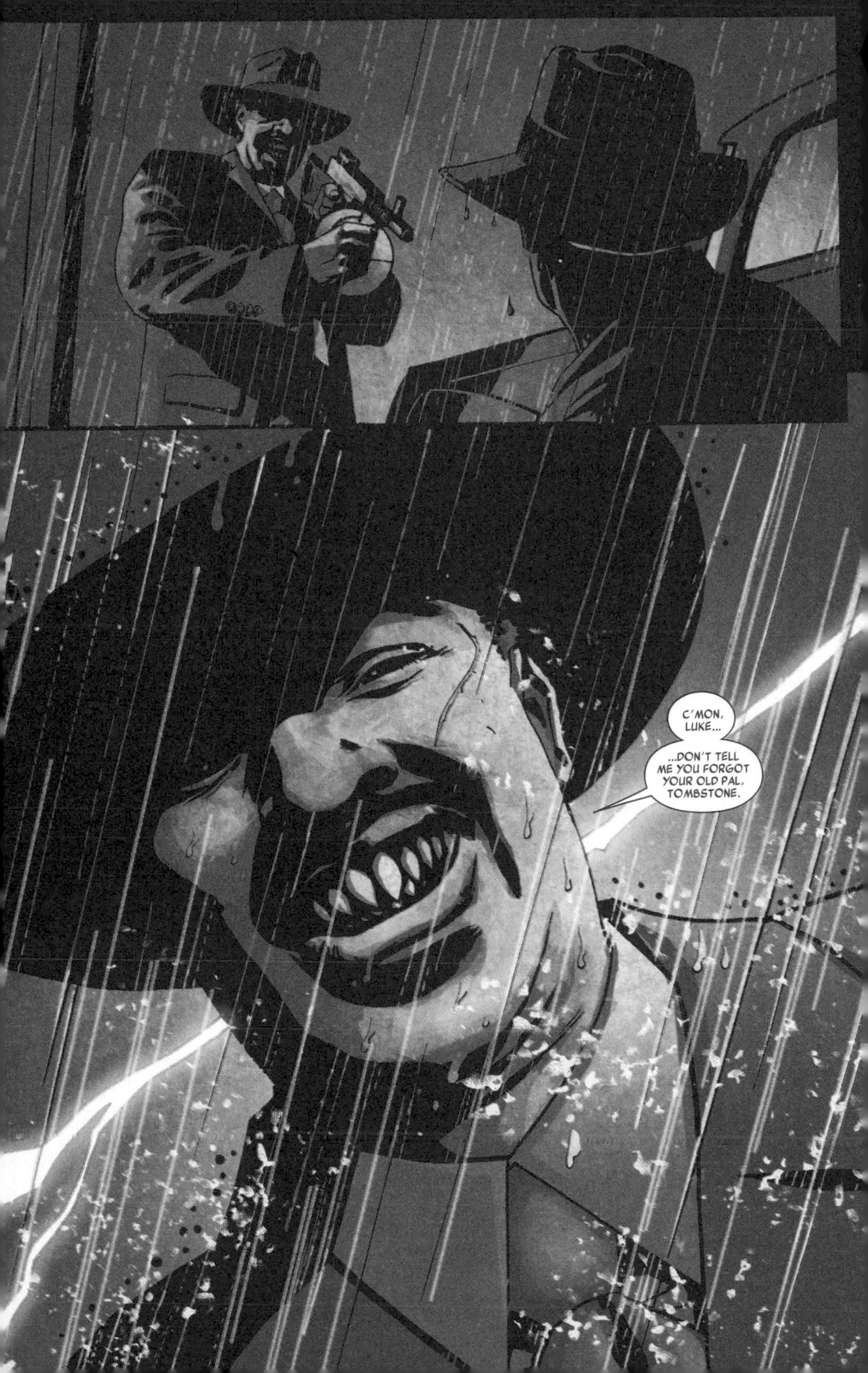
C'MON, LUKE...
...DON'T TELL ME YOU FORGOT YOUR OLD PAL, TOMBSTONE.

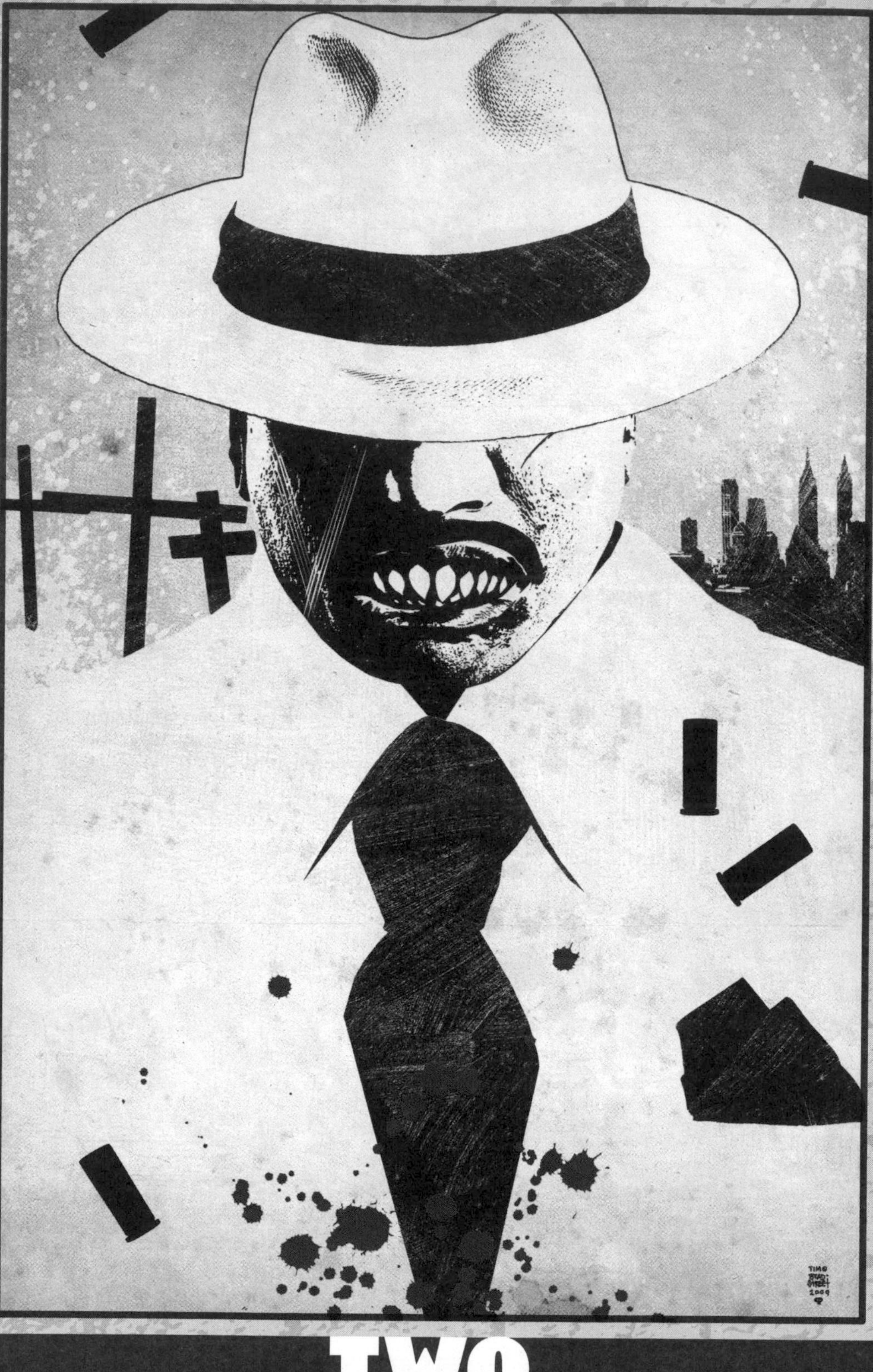

TWO

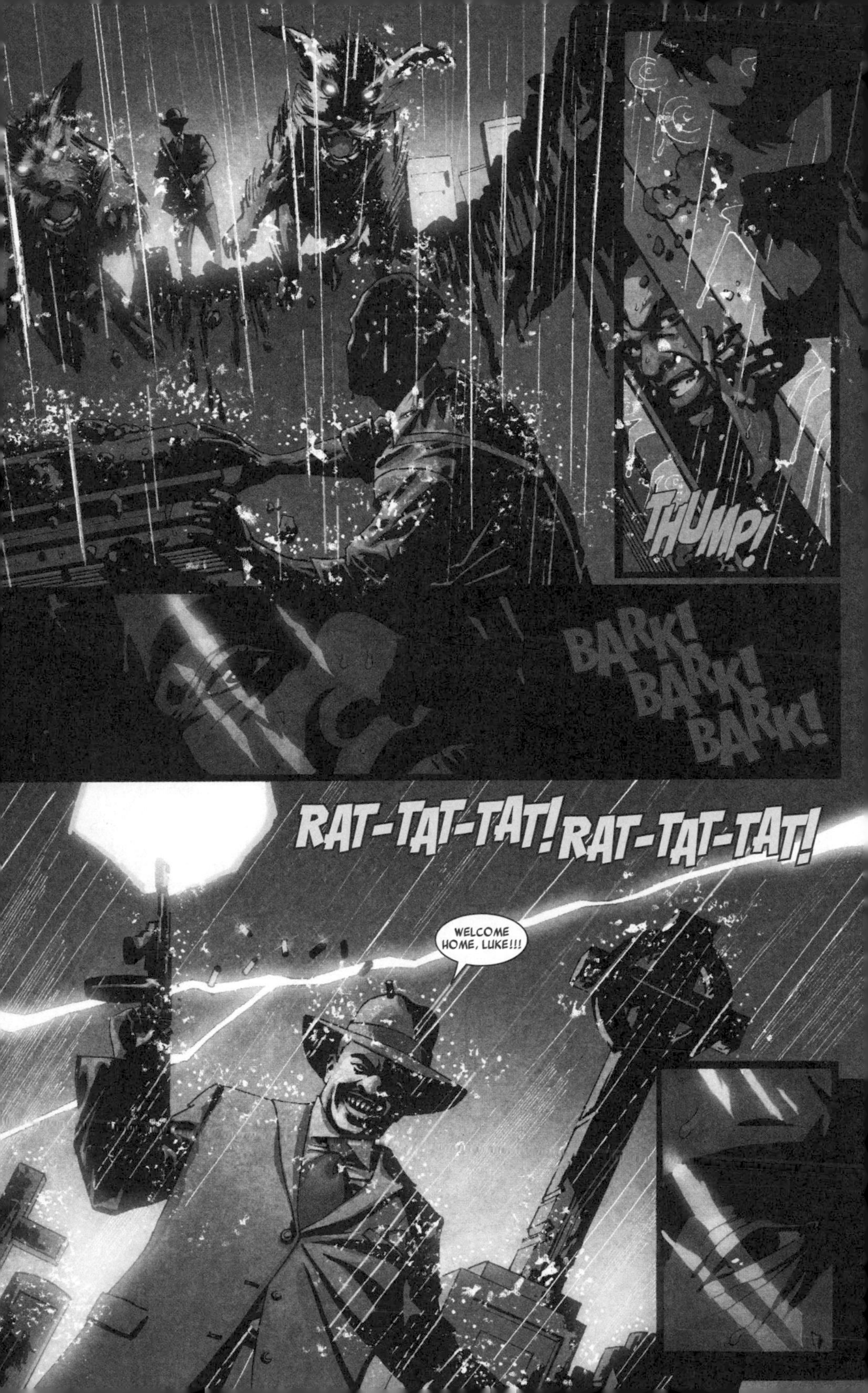
THUMP!
BARK! BARK! BARK!
RAT-TAT-TAT! RAT-TAT-TAT!
WELCOME HOME, LUKE!!!

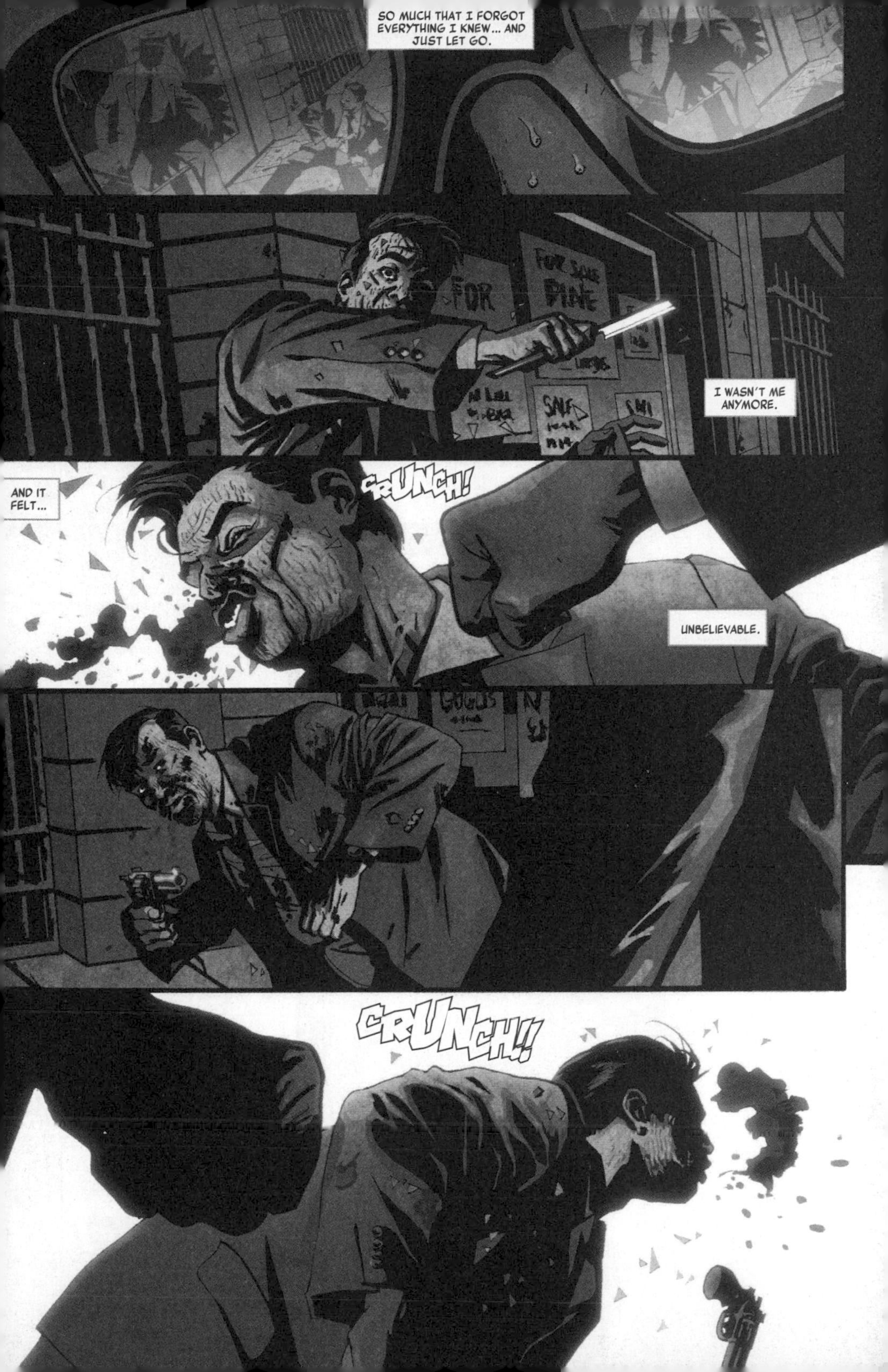
SO MUCH THAT I FORGOT EVERYTHING I KNEW... AND JUST LET GO.
I WASN'T ME ANYMORE.
AND IT FELT...
CRUNCH!
UNBELIEVABLE.
CRUNCH!!

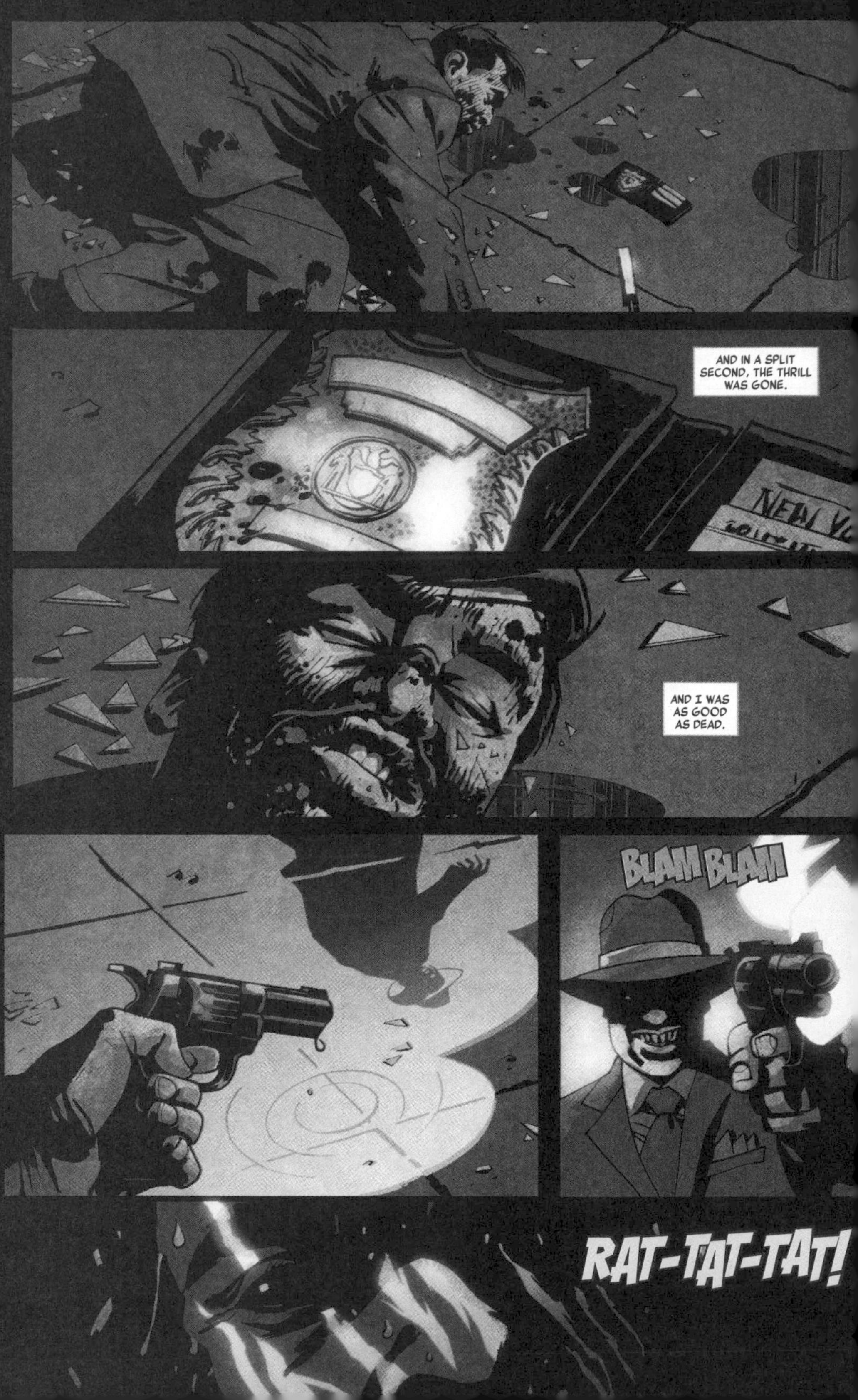
AND IN A SPLIT SECOND, THE THRILL WAS GONE.
AND I WAS AS GOOD AS DEAD.
BLAM BLAM
RAT-TAT-TAT!

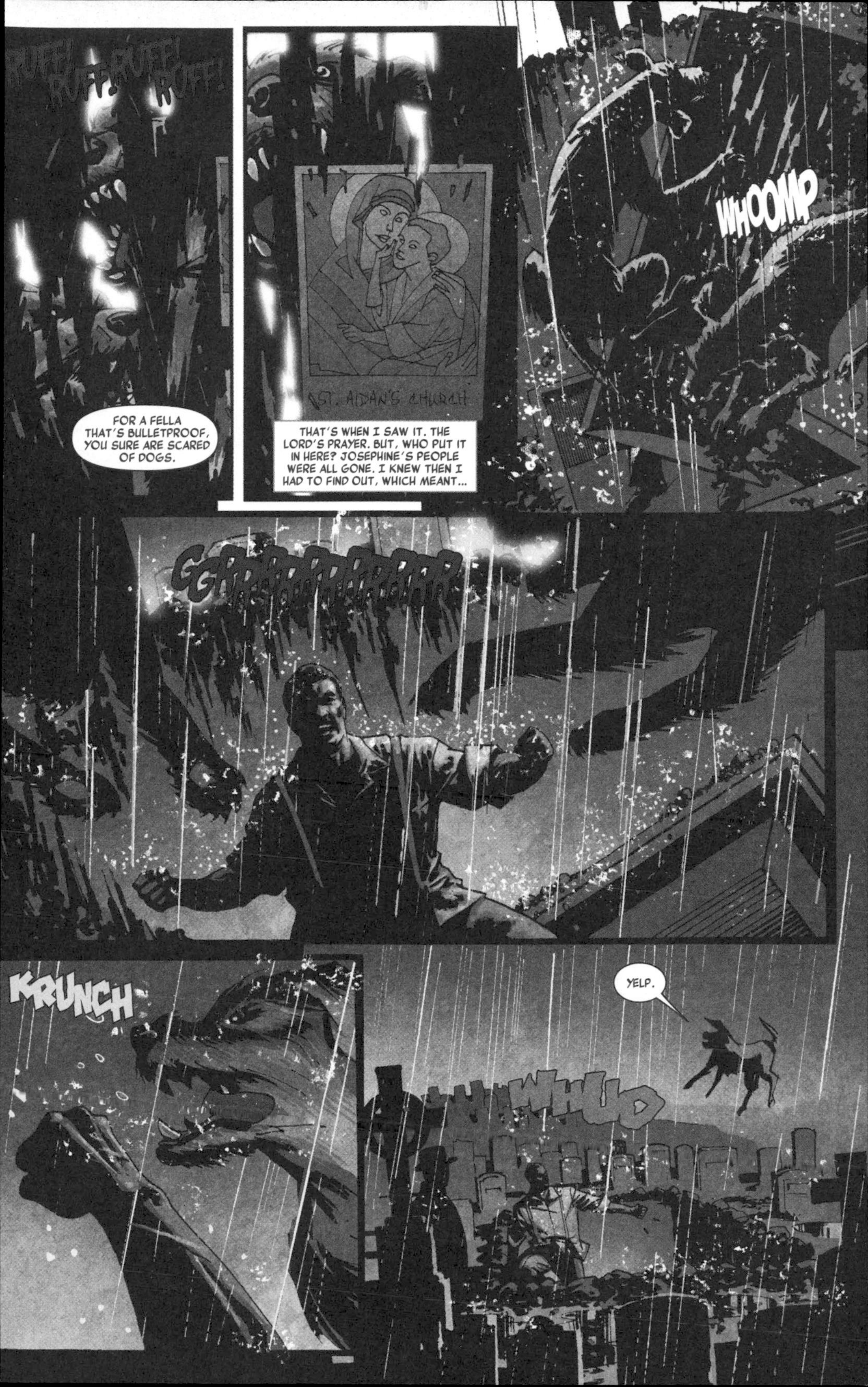
RUFF! RUFF! RUFF! RUFF!
ST. AIDAN'S CHURCH
FOR A FELLA THAT'S BULLETPROOF, YOU SURE ARE SCARED OF DOGS.
THAT'S WHEN I SAW IT. THE LORD'S PRAYER. BUT, WHO PUT IT IN HERE? JOSEPHINE'S PEOPLE WERE ALL GONE. I KNEW THEN I HAD TO FIND OUT, WHICH MEANT...
WHOOMP
GGRRRRRRRRRRRR
KRUNCH
YELP.
WHHHWHUO

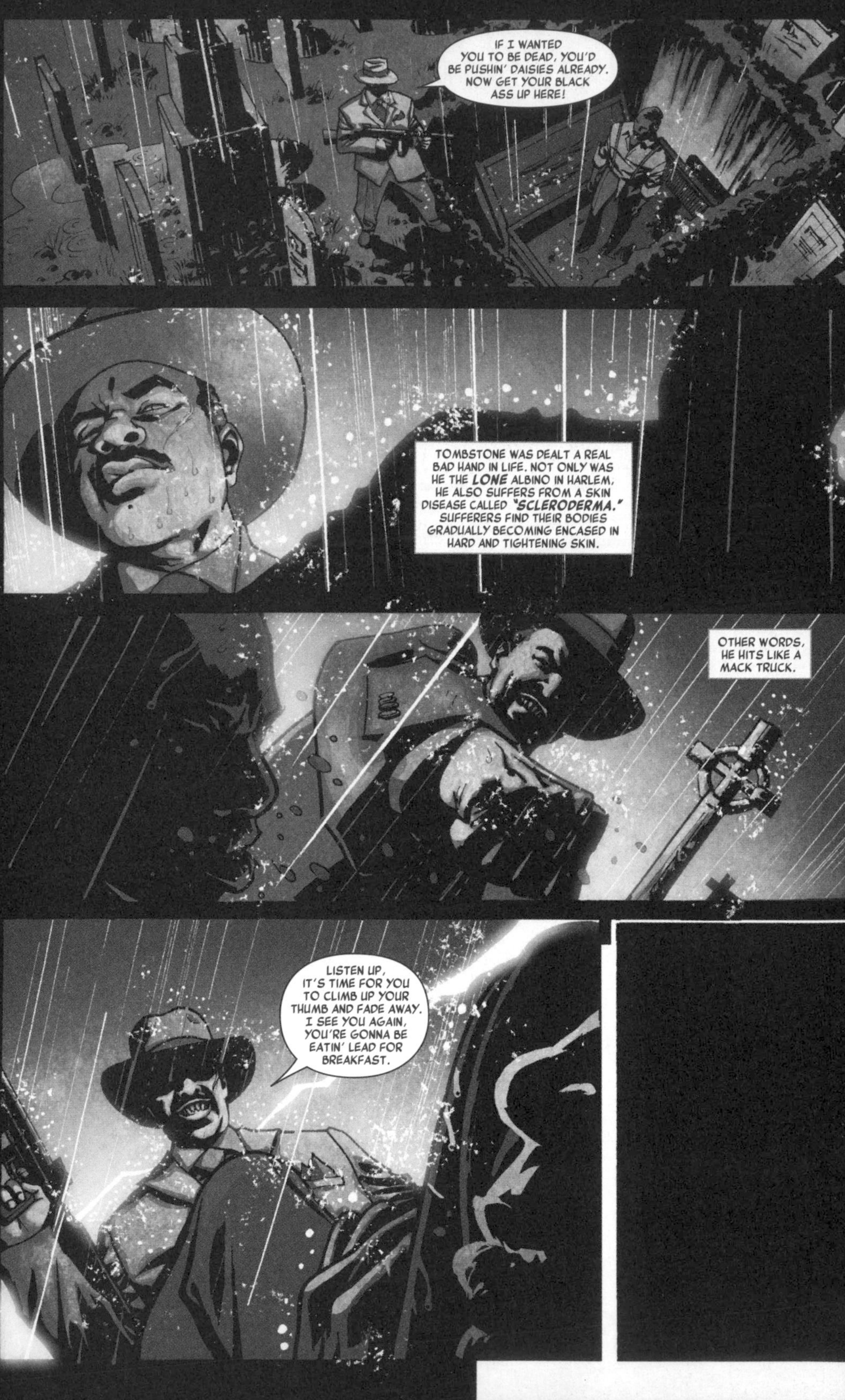
IF I WANTED YOU TO BE DEAD, YOU'D BE PUSHIN' DAISIES ALREADY. NOW GET YOUR BLACK ASS UP HERE!
TOMBSTONE WAS DEALT A REAL BAD HAND IN LIFE. NOT ONLY WAS HE THE LONE ALBINO IN HARLEM, HE ALSO SUFFERS FROM A SKIN DISEASE CALLED "SCLERODERMA." SUFFERERS FIND THEIR BODIES GRADUALLY BECOMING ENCASED IN HARD AND TIGHTENING SKIN.
OTHER WORDS, HE HITS LIKE A MACK TRUCK.
LISTEN UP, IT'S TIME FOR YOU TO CLIMB UP YOUR THUMB AND FADE AWAY. I SEE YOU AGAIN, YOU'RE GONNA BE EATIN' LEAD FOR BREAKFAST.

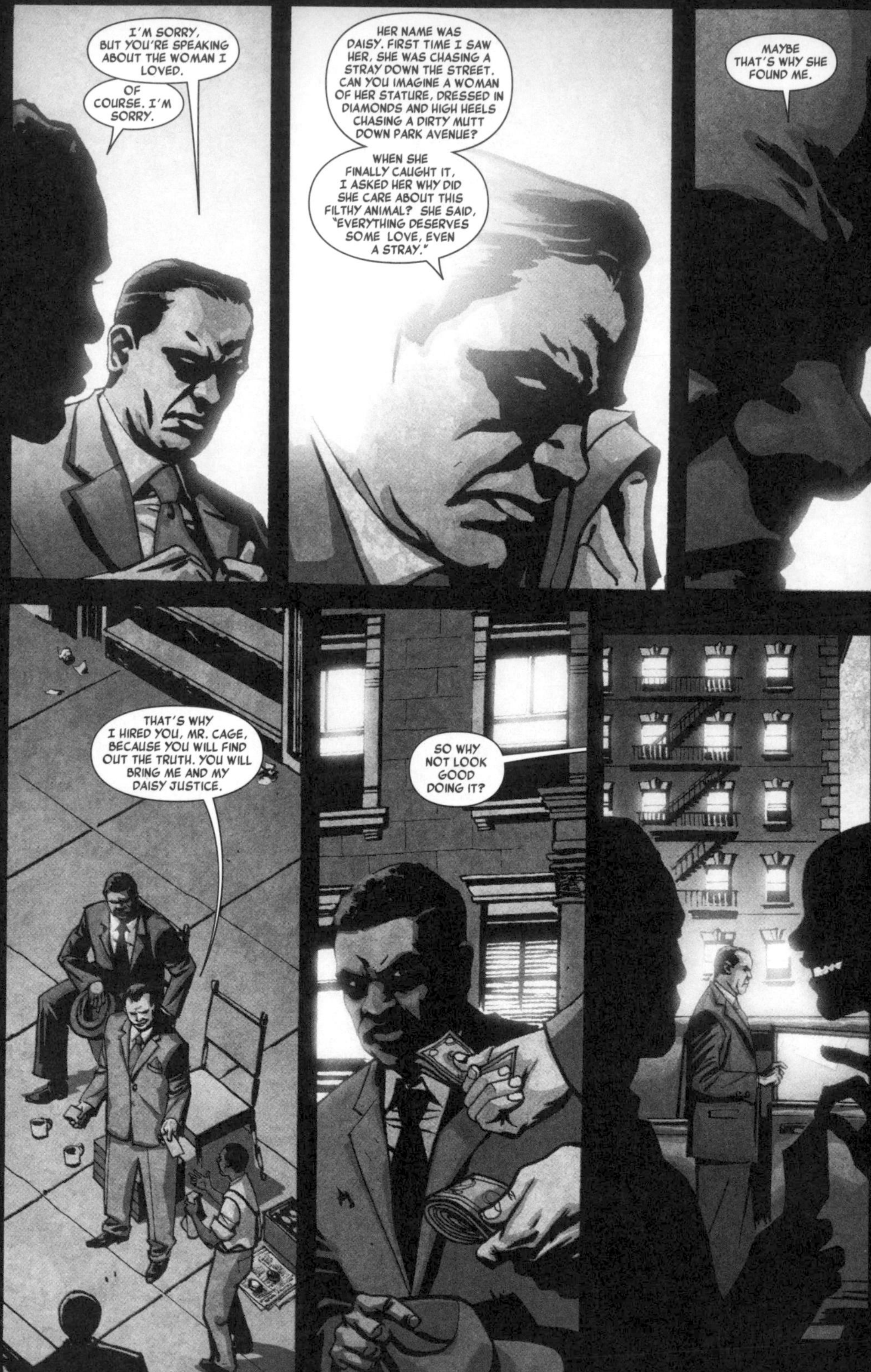
I'M SORRY, BUT YOU'RE SPEAKING ABOUT THE WOMAN I LOVED.
OF COURSE. I'M SORRY.
HER NAME WAS DAISY. FIRST TIME I SAW HER, SHE WAS CHASING A STRAY DOWN THE STREET. CAN YOU IMAGINE A WOMAN OF HER STATURE, DRESSED IN DIAMONDS AND HIGH HEELS CHASING A DIRTY MUTT DOWN PARK AVENUE?
WHEN SHE FINALLY CAUGHT IT, I ASKED HER WHY DID SHE CARE ABOUT THIS FILTHY ANIMAL? SHE SAID, "EVERYTHING DESERVES SOME LOVE, EVEN A STRAY."
MAYBE THAT'S WHY SHE FOUND ME.
THAT'S WHY I HIRED YOU, MR. CAGE, BECAUSE YOU WILL FIND OUT THE TRUTH. YOU WILL BRING ME AND MY DAISY JUSTICE.
SO WHY NOT LOOK GOOD DOING IT?

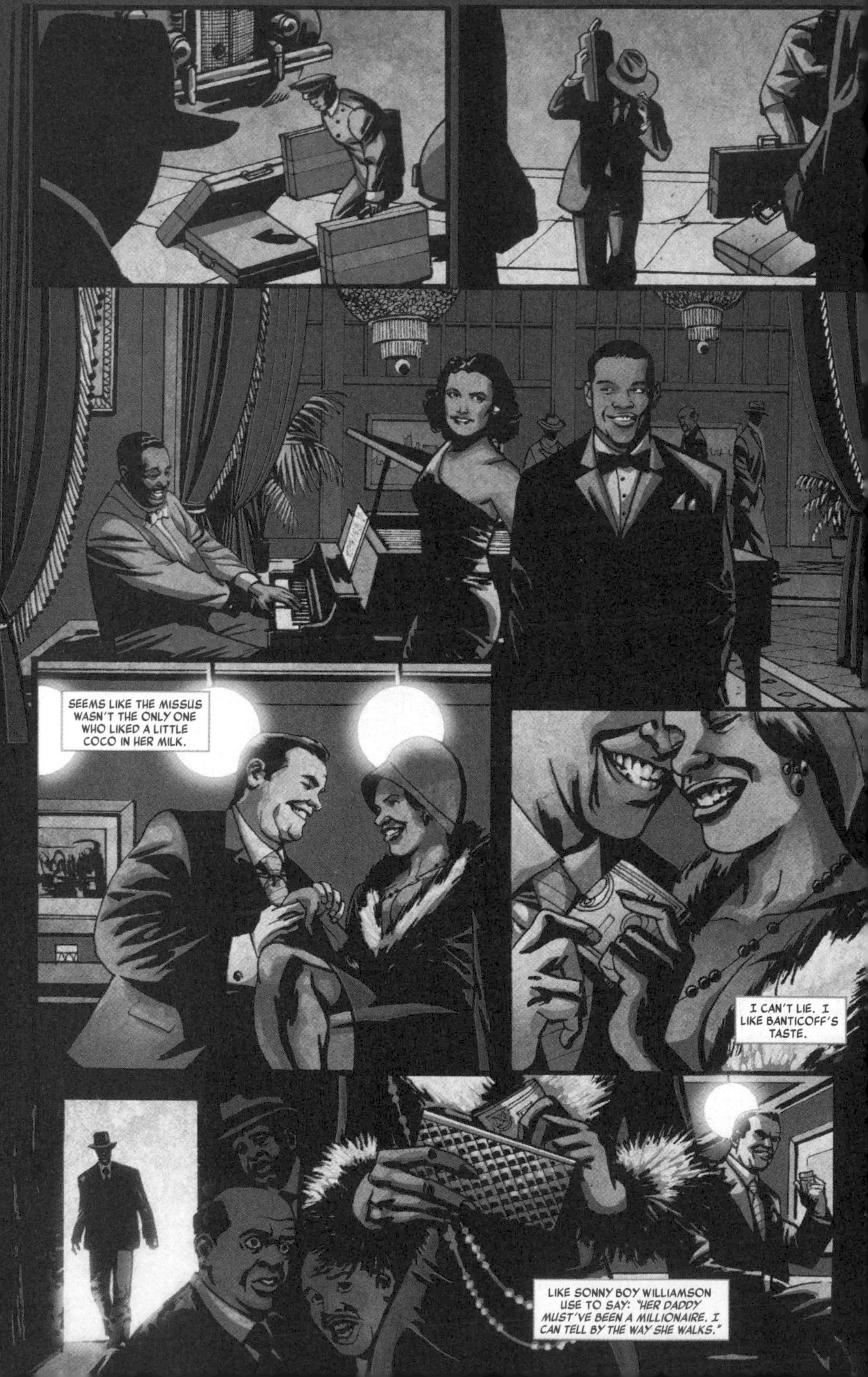
SEEMS LIKE THE MISSUS WASN'T THE ONLY ONE WHO LIKED A LITTLE COCO IN HER MILK.
I CAN'T LIE. I LIKE BANTICOFF'S TASTE.
LIKE SONNY BOY WILLIAMSON USE TO SAY: "HER DADDY MUST'VE BEEN A MILLIONAIRE. I CAN TELL BY THE WAY SHE WALKS."

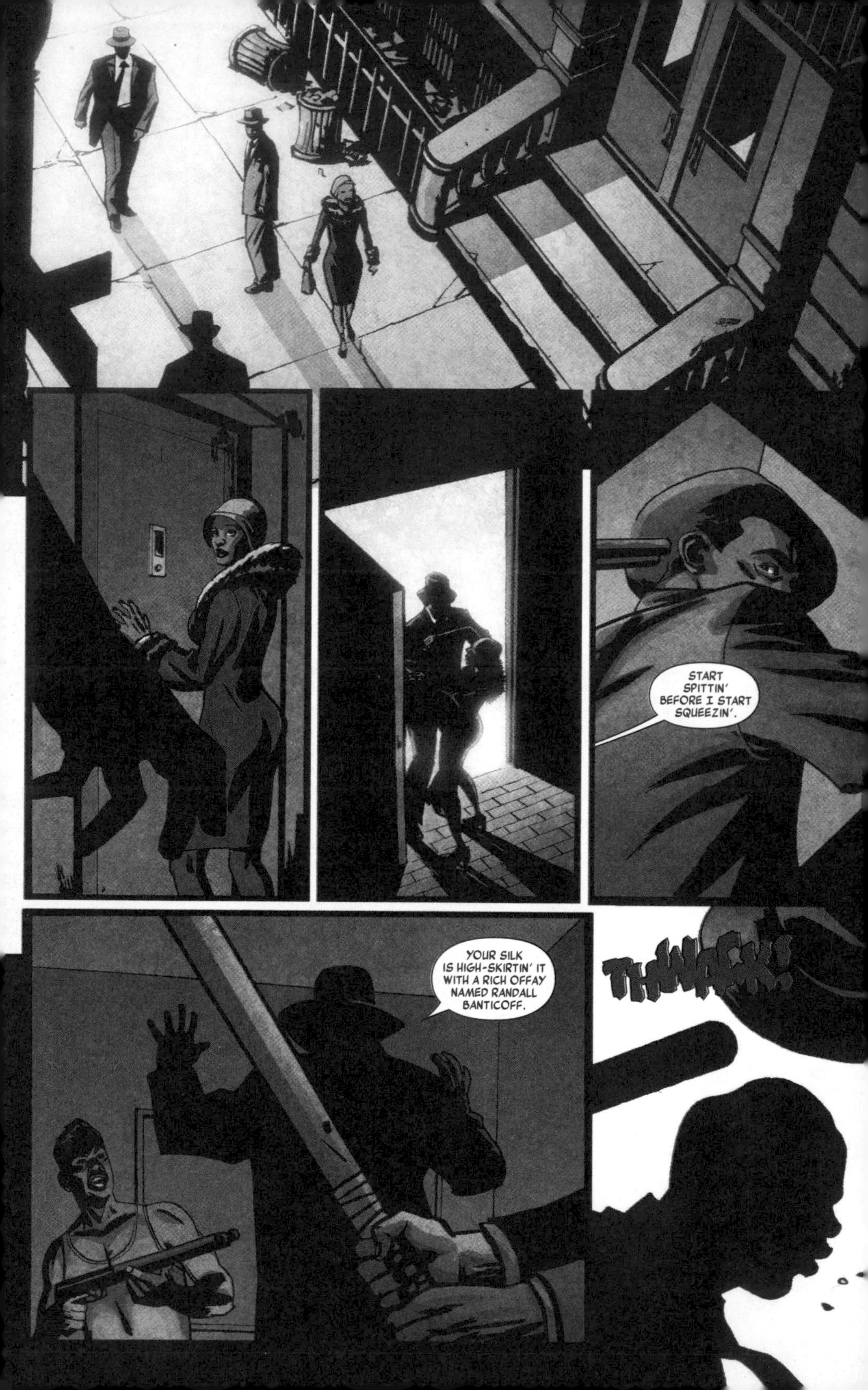
START SPITTIN' BEFORE I START SQUEEZIN'.
YOUR SILK IS HIGH-SKIRTIN' IT WITH A RICH OFFAY NAMED RANDALL BANTICOFF.
THWACK!

LAST TIME MY DOME HURT LIKE THIS IT INVOLVED TWO SHOWGIRLS FROM THE SAVOY ROOM AND A BOTTLE OF CORN LIQUOR.

KNOCK! KNOCK! KNOCK!

POLICE! OPEN UP!

THAT'S WHEN IT HIT ME LIKE A BAG OF NICKELS:

I WAS BEING SET UP.

LEASE

This Residential Lease shall evidence the terms and conditions which the parties whose signatures appear below have agreed.

Tenant(s)/Lessee, *Luke Cage*, shall be referred to as "RESIDENT". As consideration for this agreement, OWNER agrees to rent/lease to RESIDENT and RESIDENT agrees to rent/lease from OWNER solely as a private residence.

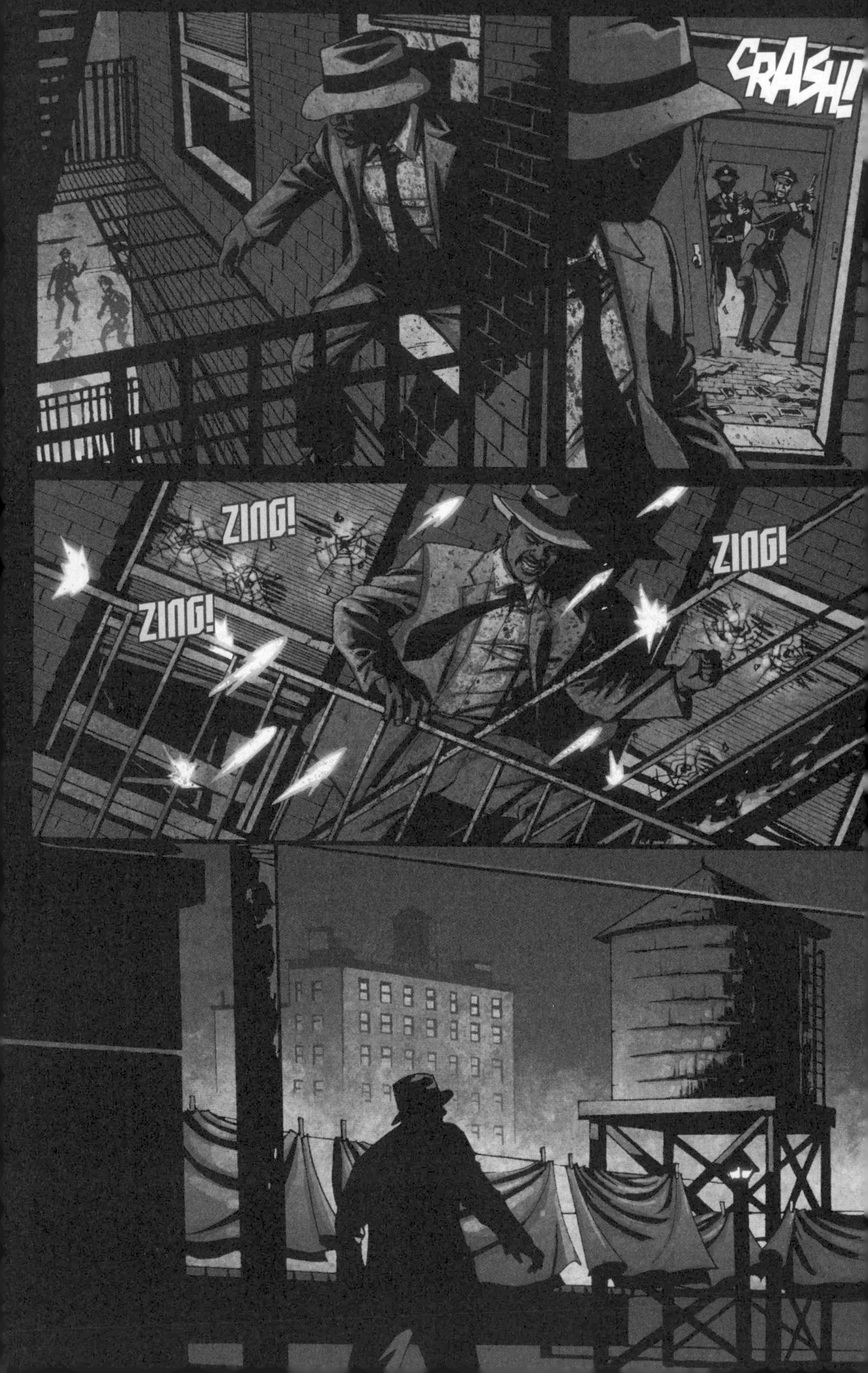
CRASH!
ZING!
ZING!
ZING!

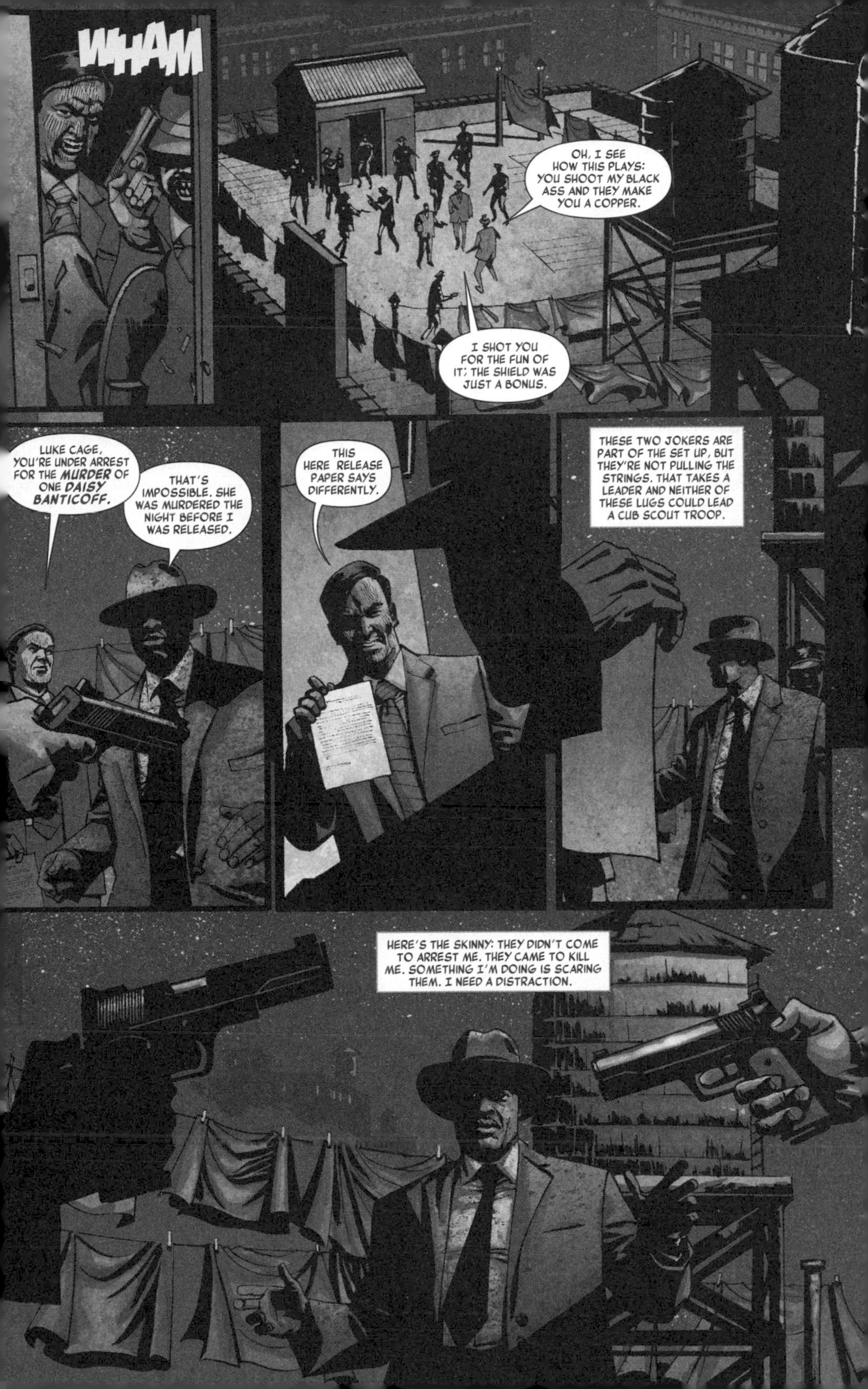
WHAM
OH, I SEE HOW THIS PLAYS: YOU SHOOT MY BLACK ASS AND THEY MAKE YOU A COPPER.
I SHOT YOU FOR THE FUN OF IT; THE SHIELD WAS JUST A BONUS.
LUKE CAGE, YOU'RE UNDER ARREST FOR THE **MURDER** OF ONE **DAISY BANTICOFF**.
THAT'S IMPOSSIBLE. SHE WAS MURDERED THE NIGHT BEFORE I WAS RELEASED.
THIS HERE RELEASE PAPER SAYS DIFFERENTLY.
THESE TWO JOKERS ARE PART OF THE SET UP, BUT THEY'RE NOT PULLING THE STRINGS. THAT TAKES A LEADER AND NEITHER OF THESE LUGS COULD LEAD A CUB SCOUT TROOP.
HERE'S THE SKINNY: THEY DIDN'T COME TO ARREST ME. THEY CAME TO KILL ME. SOMETHING I'M DOING IS SCARING THEM. I NEED A DISTRACTION.

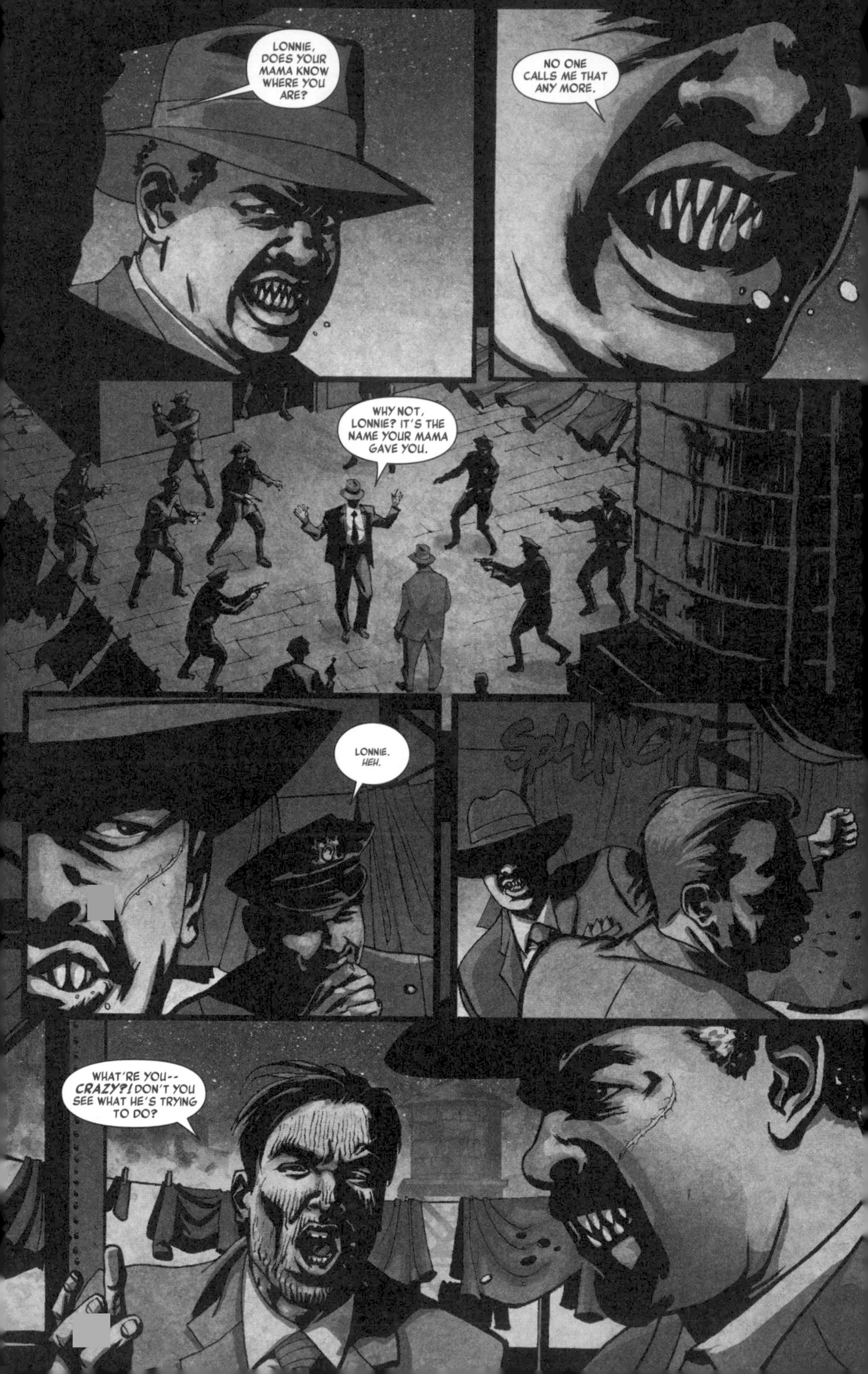

LONNIE, DOES YOUR MAMA KNOW WHERE YOU ARE?
NO ONE CALLS ME THAT ANY MORE.
WHY NOT, LONNIE? IT'S THE NAME YOUR MAMA GAVE YOU.
LONNIE. HEH.
WHAT'RE YOU-- CRAZY?! DON'T YOU SEE WHAT HE'S TRYING TO DO?

ONLY THIS BRICK WALL PUNCHES BACK.
KAPUSH!
WHUD
IS THAT YOUR BEST SHOT?
NOPE.
THIS IS.
BLAM
BLAM
BLAM
BLAM

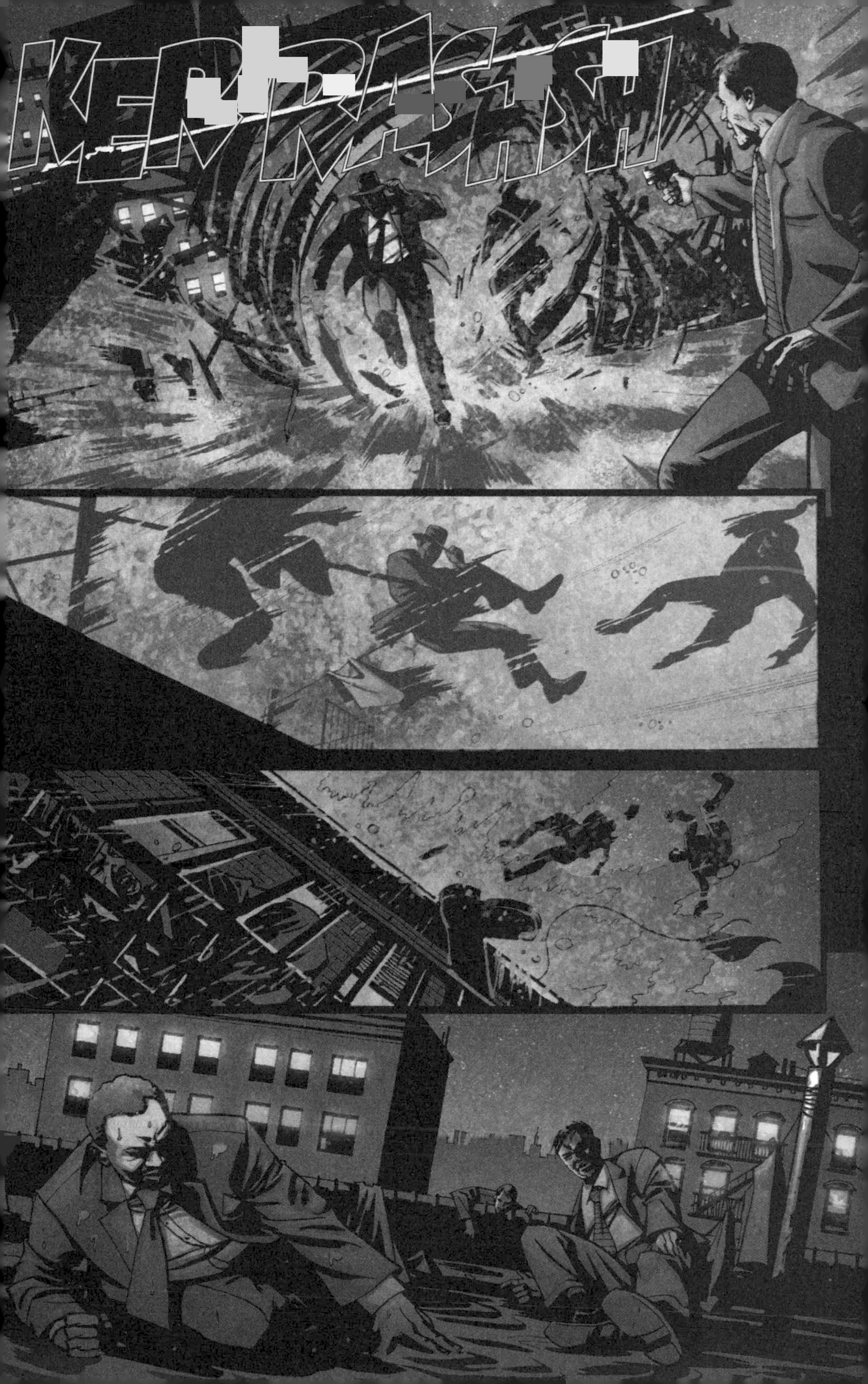

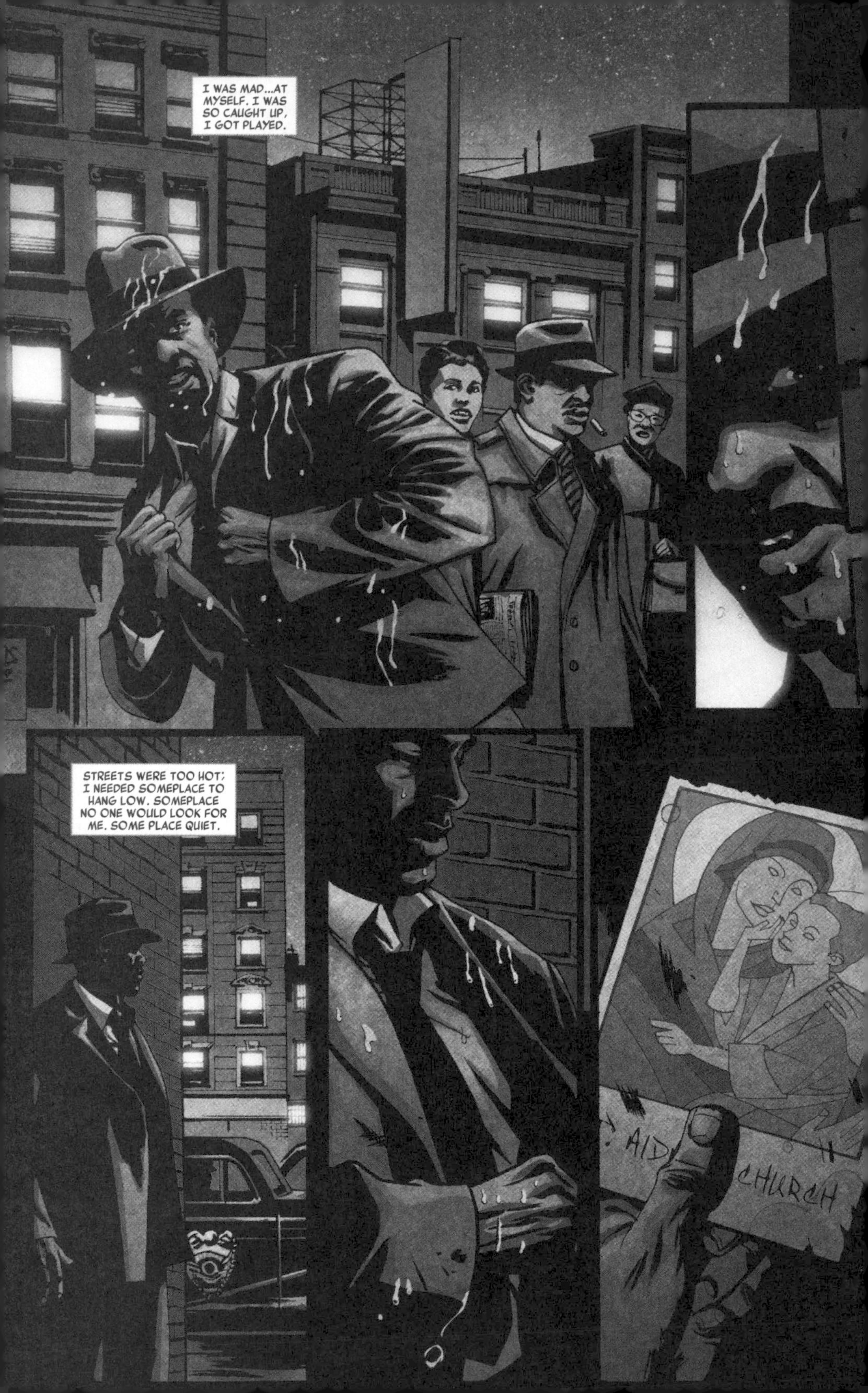
I WAS MAD...AT MYSELF. I WAS SO CAUGHT UP, I GOT PLAYED.
STREETS WERE TOO HOT; I NEEDED SOMEPLACE TO HANG LOW. SOMEPLACE NO ONE WOULD LOOK FOR ME. SOME PLACE QUIET.
AID
CHURCH

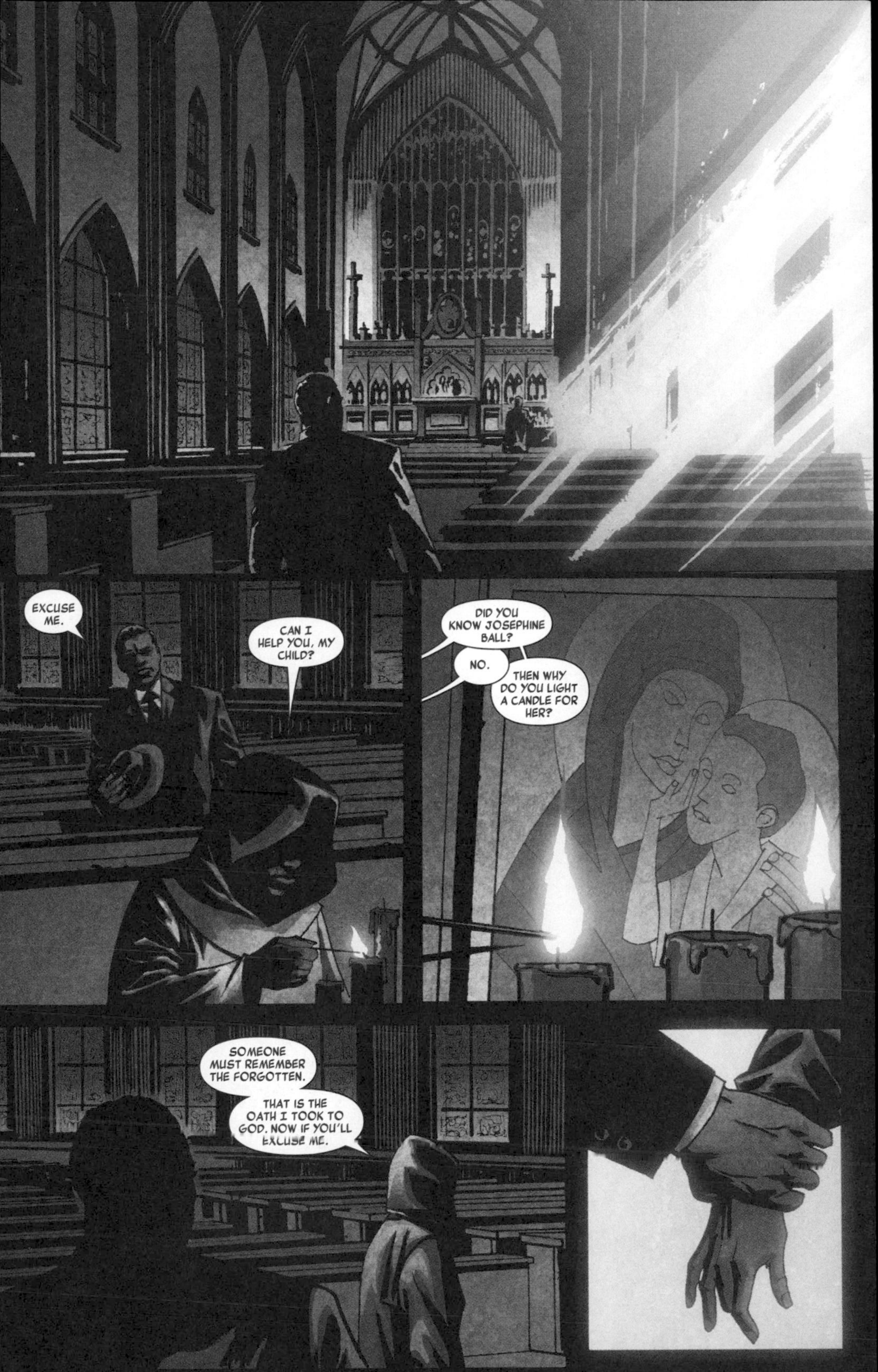
EXCUSE ME.
CAN I HELP YOU, MY CHILD?
DID YOU KNOW JOSEPHINE BALL?
NO.
THEN WHY DO YOU LIGHT A CANDLE FOR HER?
SOMEONE MUST REMEMBER THE FORGOTTEN.
THAT IS THE OATH I TOOK TO GOD. NOW IF YOU'LL EXCUSE ME.

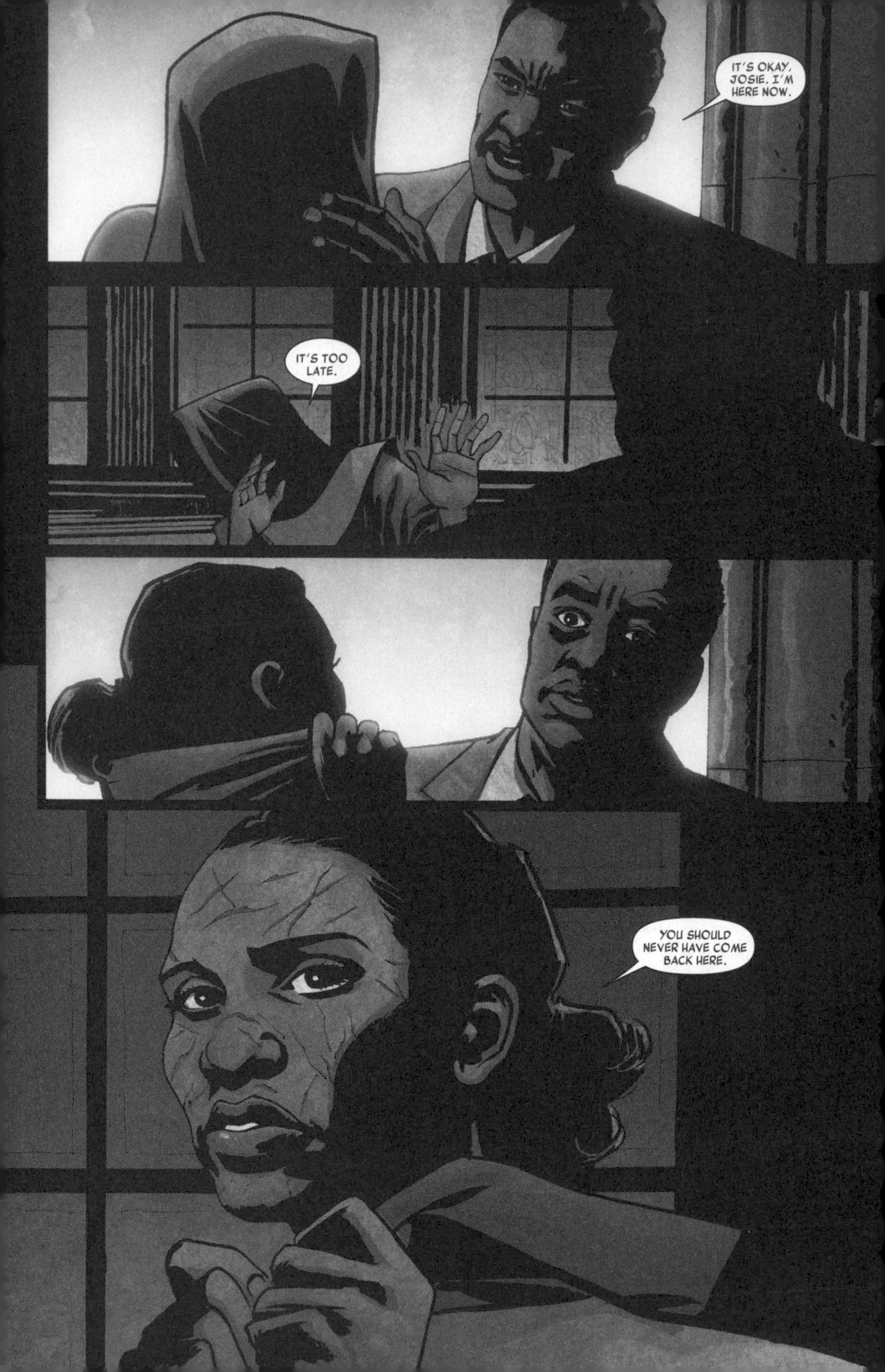
IT'S OKAY, JOSIE. I'M HERE NOW.
IT'S TOO LATE.
YOU SHOULD NEVER HAVE COME BACK HERE.

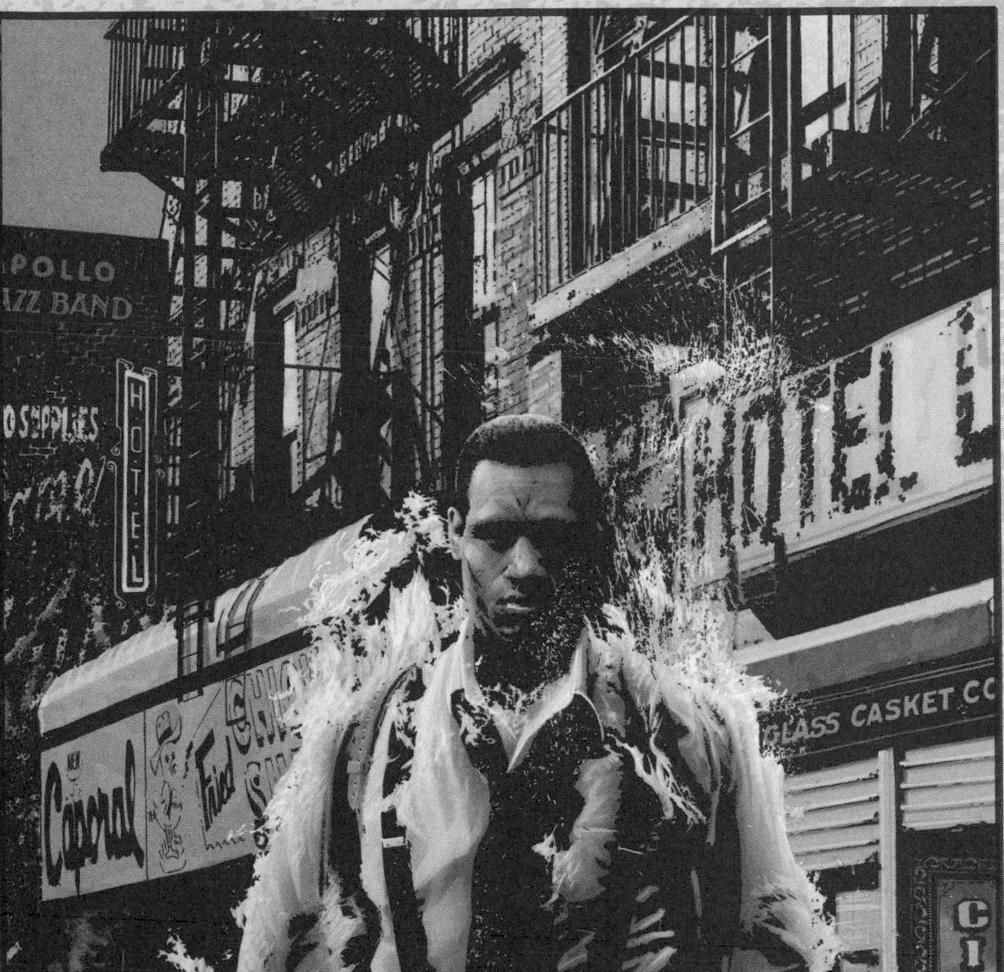
POLLO
AZZ BAND
HOTEL
GLASS CASKET CO
CIGARS

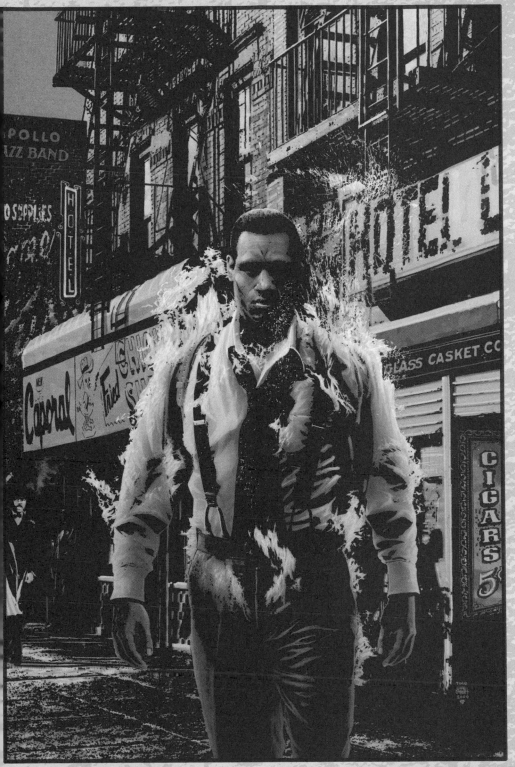

THREE

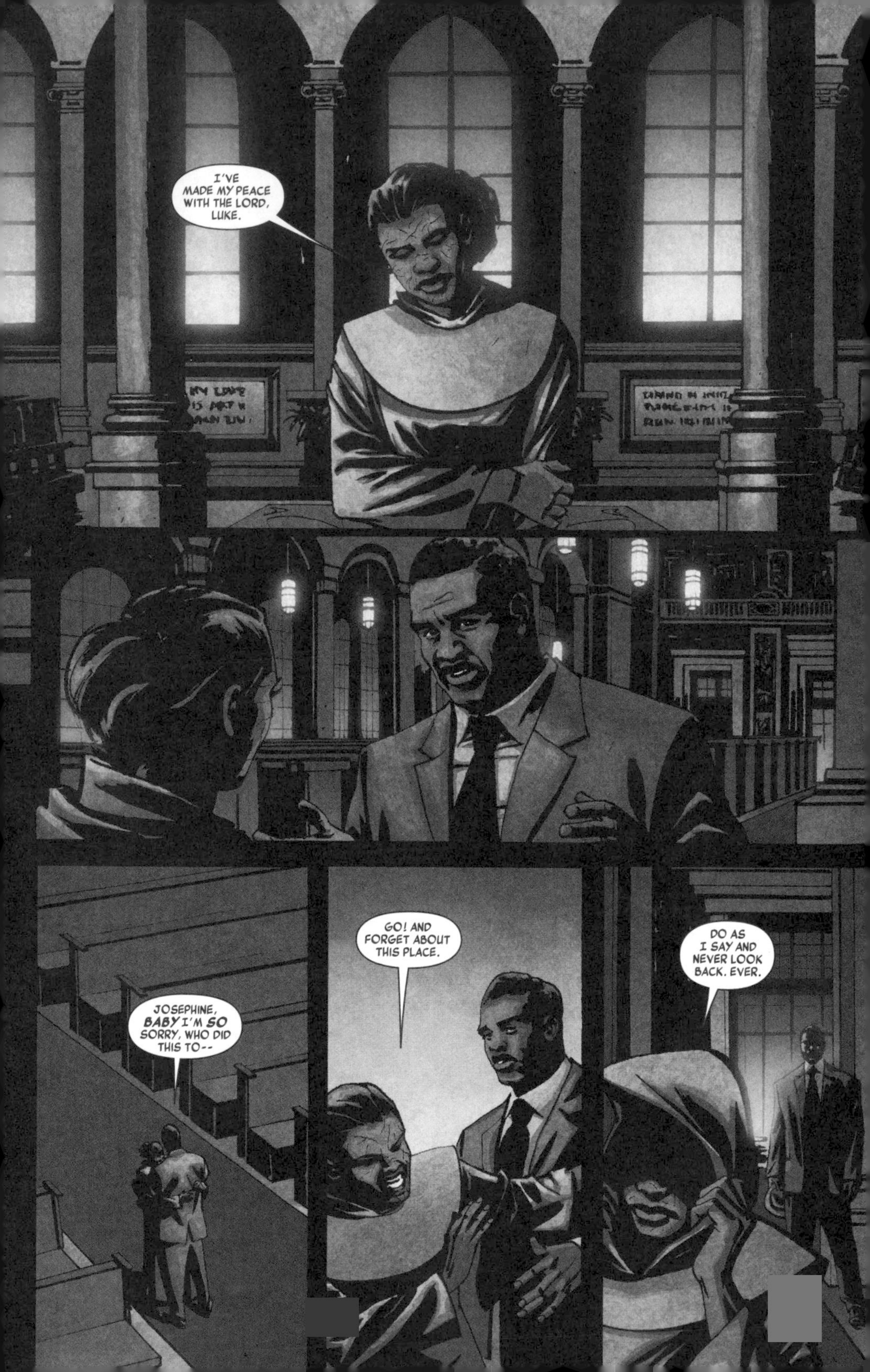
I'VE MADE MY PEACE WITH THE LORD, LUKE.
JOSEPHINE, *BABY* I'M *SO* SORRY, WHO DID THIS TO--
GO! AND FORGET ABOUT THIS PLACE.
DO AS I SAY AND NEVER LOOK BACK. EVER.

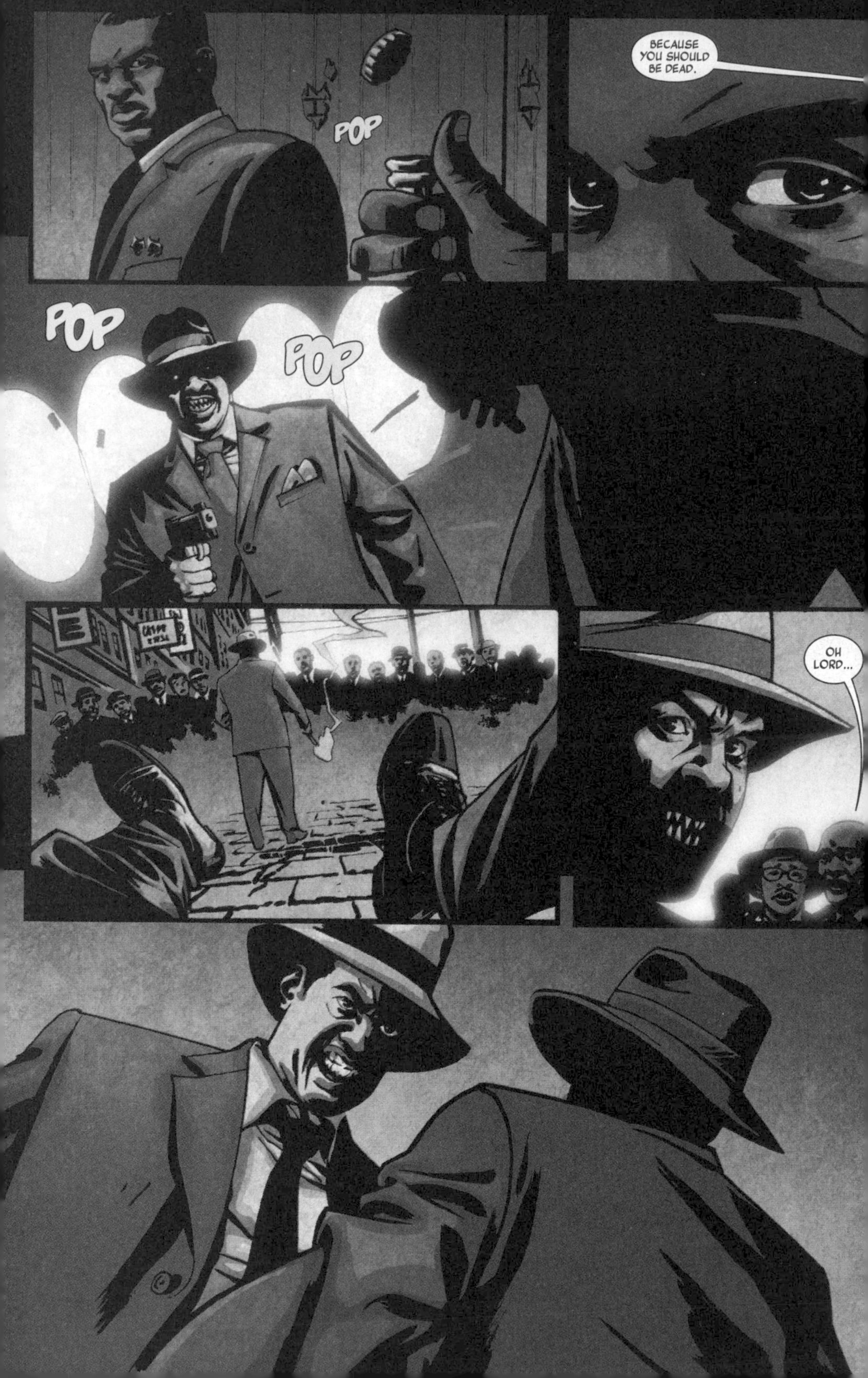
POP
BECAUSE YOU SHOULD BE DEAD.
POP
POP
OH LORD...

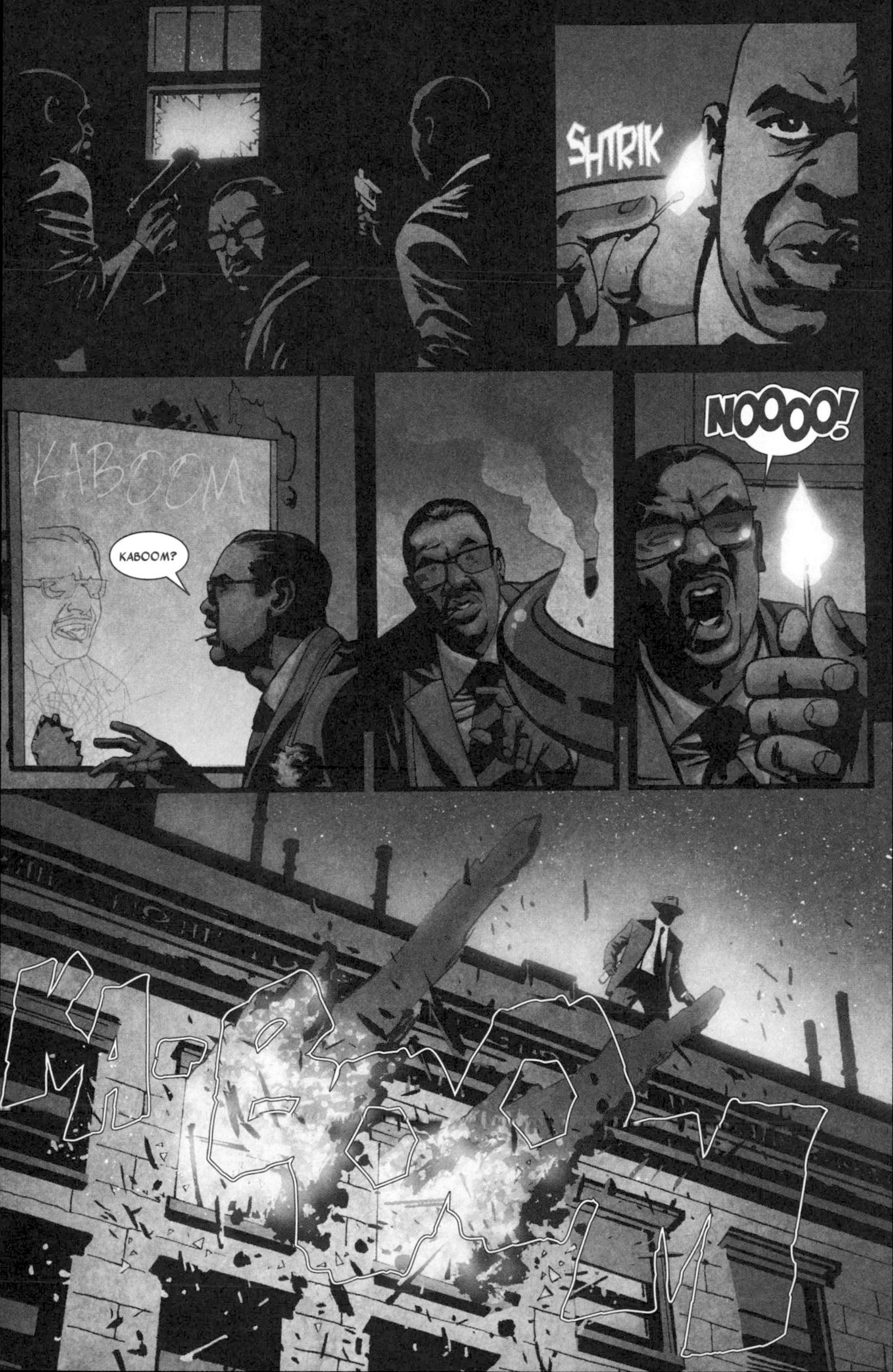
SHTRIK
KABOOM
KABOOM?
NOOOO!

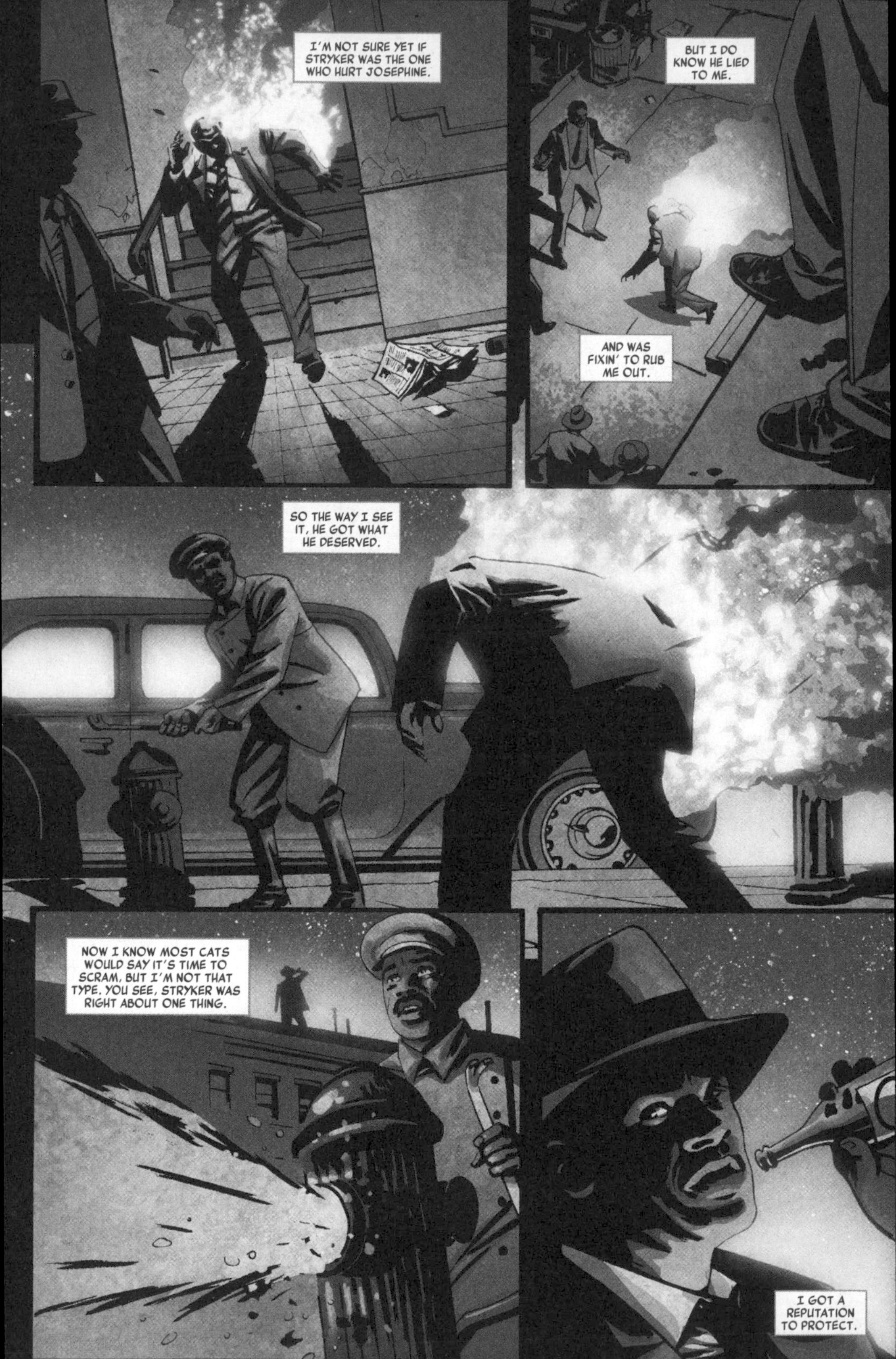
I'M NOT SURE YET IF STRYKER WAS THE ONE WHO HURT JOSEPHINE.
BUT I DO KNOW HE LIED TO ME.
AND WAS FIXIN' TO RUB ME OUT.
SO THE WAY I SEE IT, HE GOT WHAT HE DESERVED.
NOW I KNOW MOST CATS WOULD SAY IT'S TIME TO SCRAM, BUT I'M NOT THAT TYPE. YOU SEE, STRYKER WAS RIGHT ABOUT ONE THING.
I GOT A REPUTATION TO PROTECT.

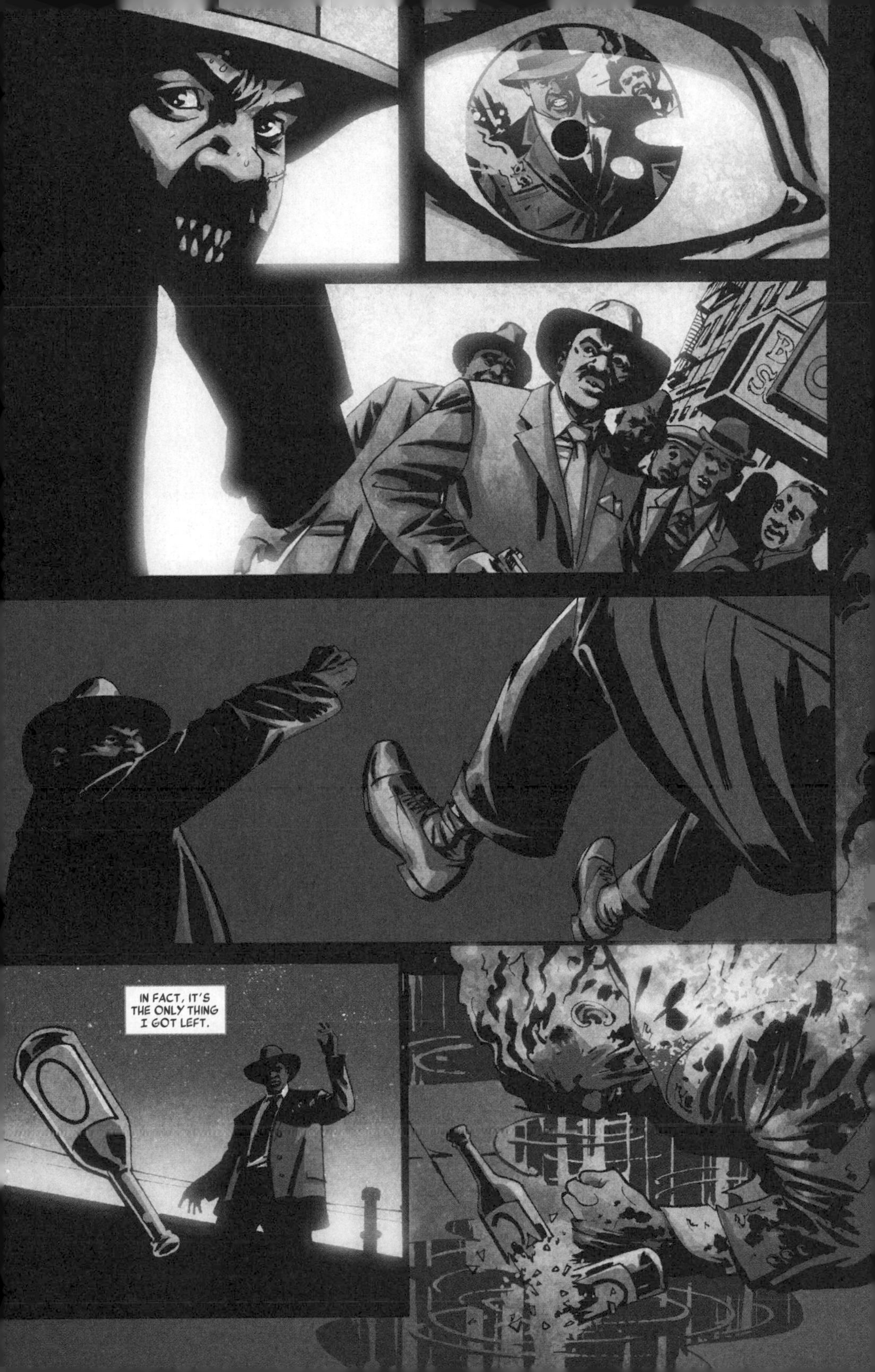
IN FACT, IT'S
THE ONLY THING
I GOT LEFT.

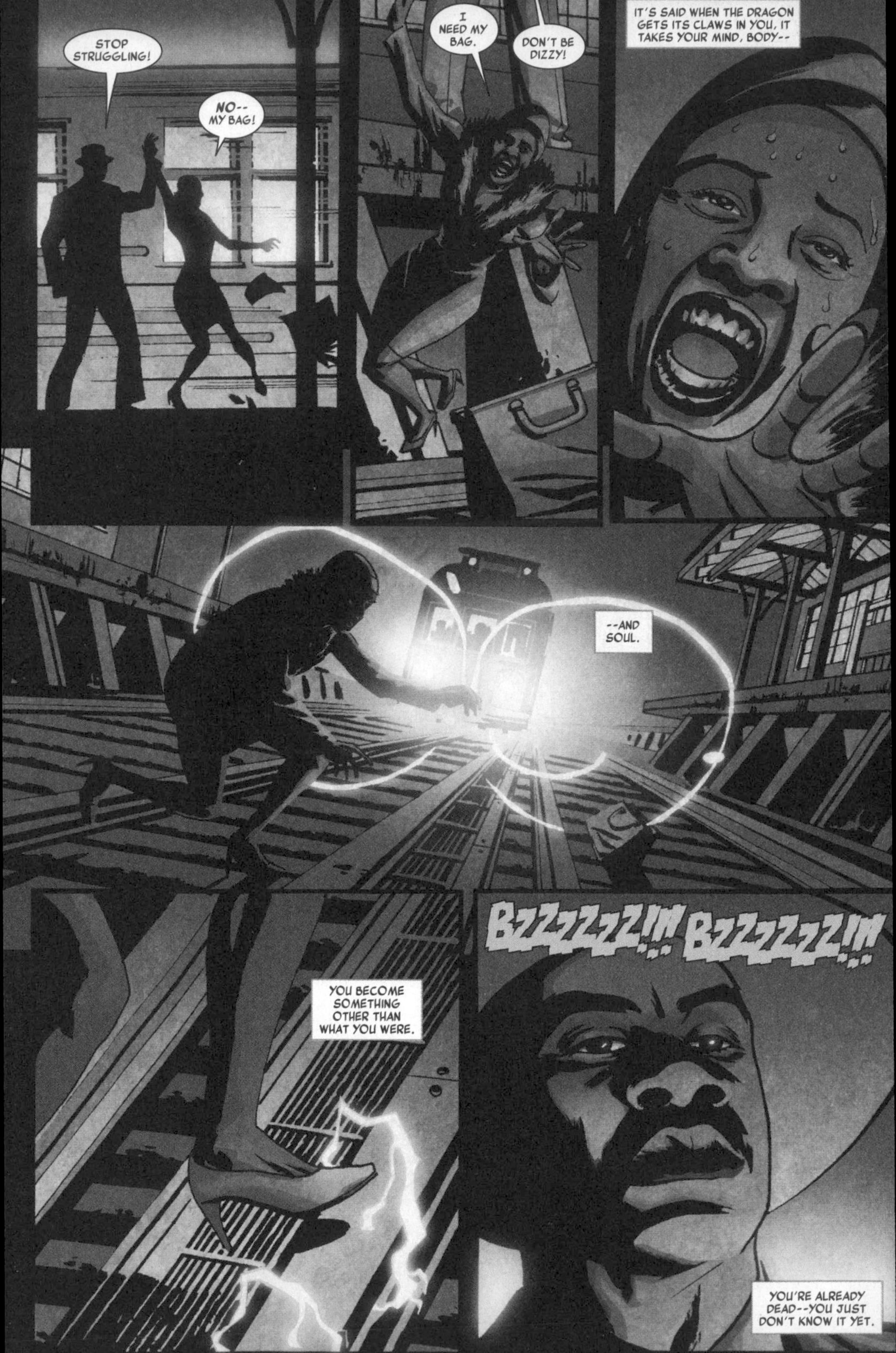
STOP STRUGGLING!
NO-- MY BAG!
I NEED MY BAG.
DON'T BE DIZZY!
IT'S SAID WHEN THE DRAGON GETS ITS CLAWS IN YOU, IT TAKES YOUR MIND, BODY--
--AND SOUL.
YOU BECOME SOMETHING OTHER THAN WHAT YOU WERE.
BZZZZZZ!!! BZZZZZZ!!!
YOU'RE ALREADY DEAD--YOU JUST DON'T KNOW IT YET.

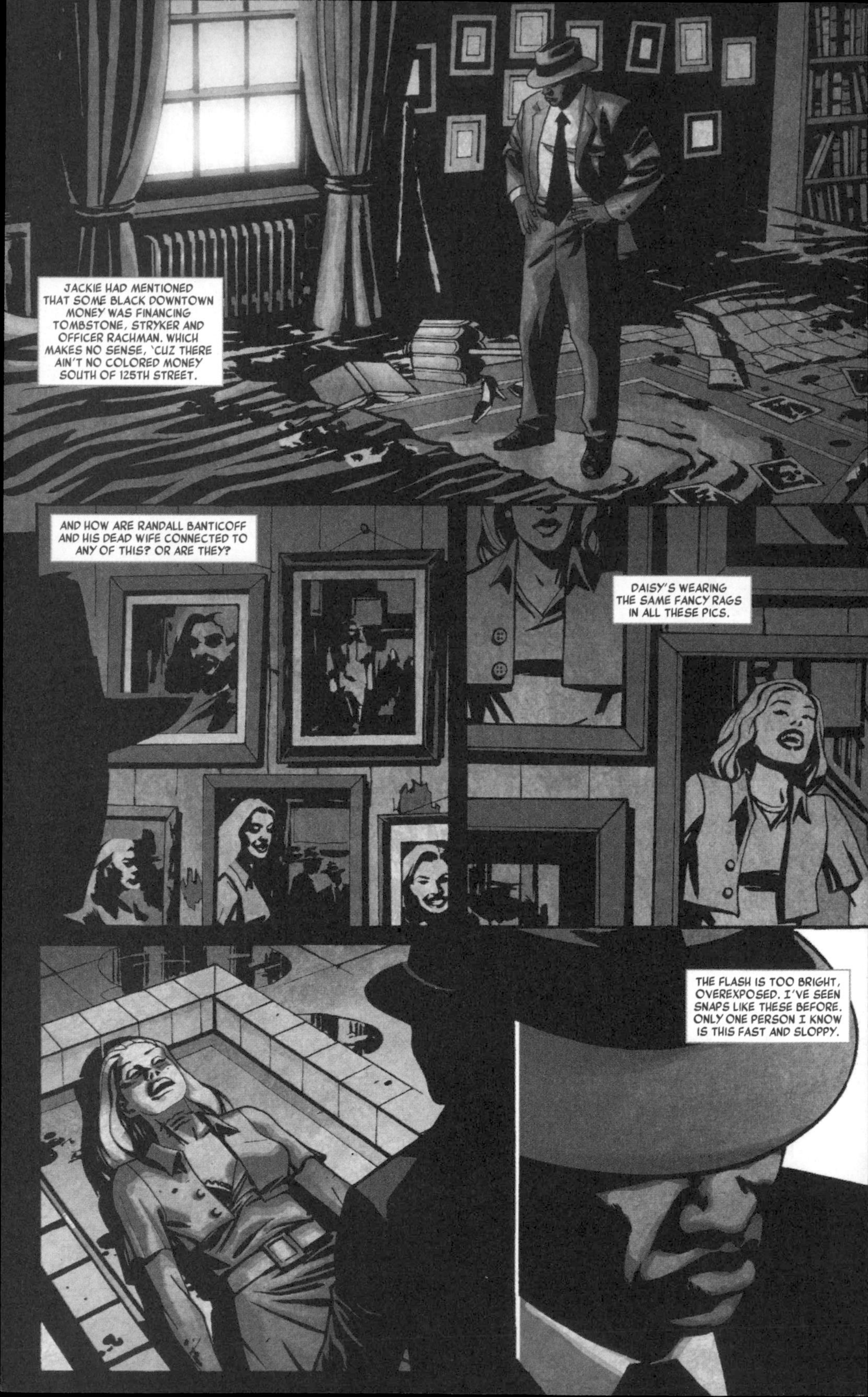
JACKIE HAD MENTIONED THAT SOME BLACK DOWNTOWN MONEY WAS FINANCING TOMBSTONE, STRYKER AND OFFICER RACHMAN. WHICH MAKES NO SENSE, 'CUZ THERE AIN'T NO COLORED MONEY SOUTH OF 125TH STREET.
AND HOW ARE RANDALL BANTICOFF AND HIS DEAD WIFE CONNECTED TO ANY OF THIS? OR ARE THEY?
DAISY'S WEARING THE SAME FANCY RAGS IN ALL THESE PICS.
THE FLASH IS TOO BRIGHT, OVEREXPOSED. I'VE SEEN SNAPS LIKE THESE BEFORE. ONLY ONE PERSON I KNOW IS THIS FAST AND SLOPPY.

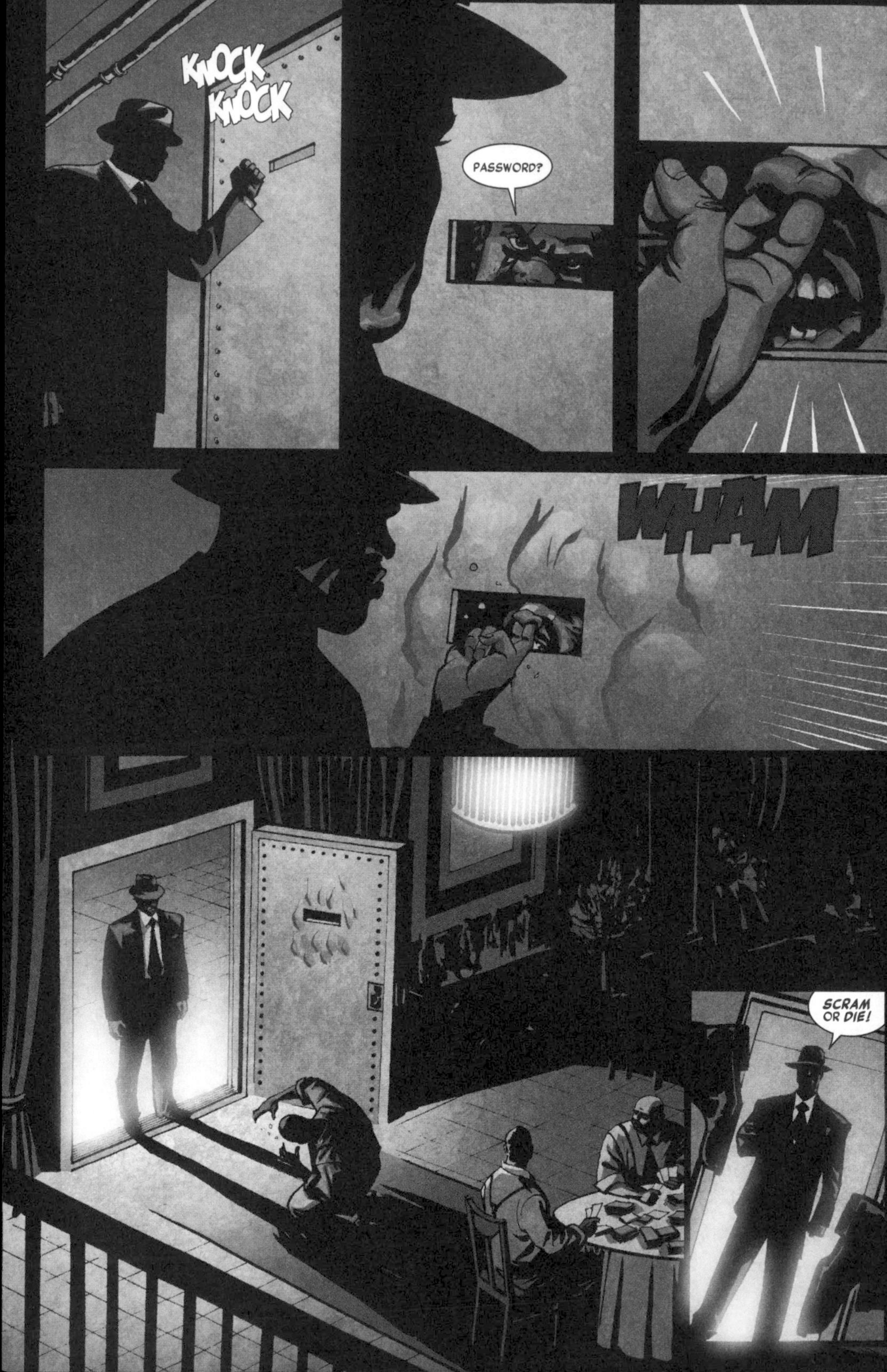
KNOCK
KNOCK
PASSWORD?
WHAM
SCRAM OR DIE!

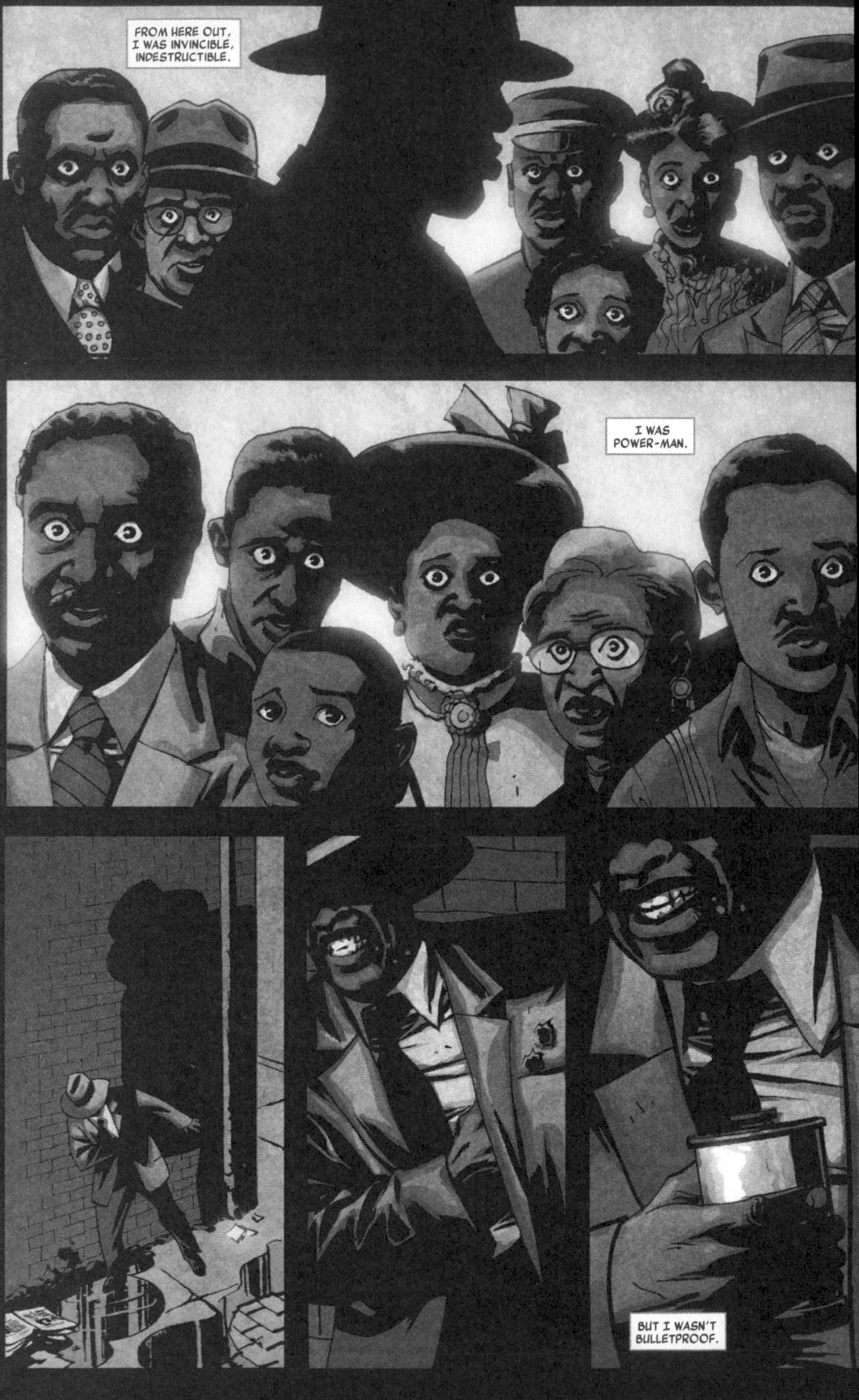
FROM HERE OUT, I WAS INVINCIBLE, INDESTRUCTIBLE.
I WAS POWER-MAN.
BUT I WASN'T BULLETPROOF.

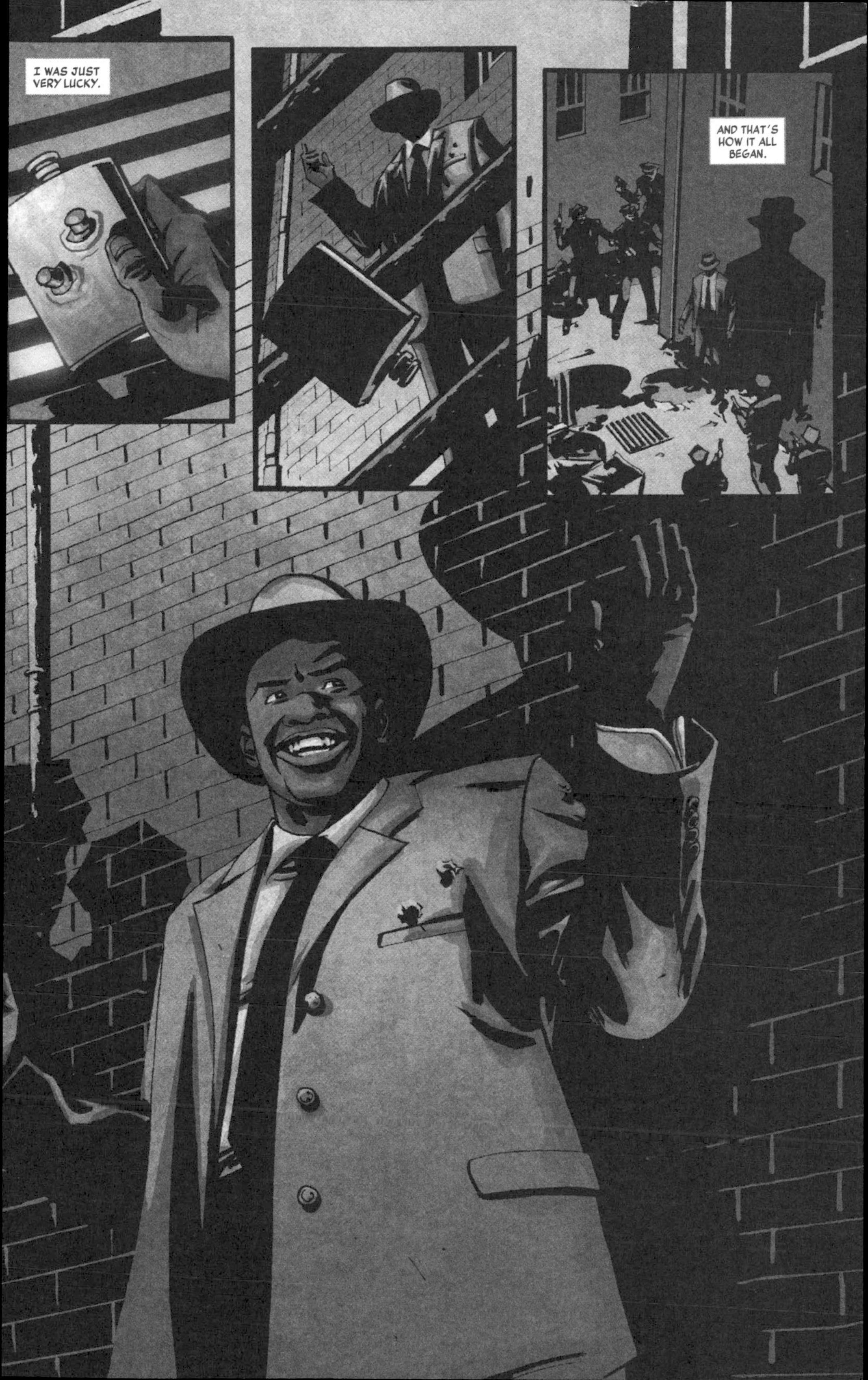
I WAS JUST VERY LUCKY.
AND THAT'S HOW IT ALL BEGAN.

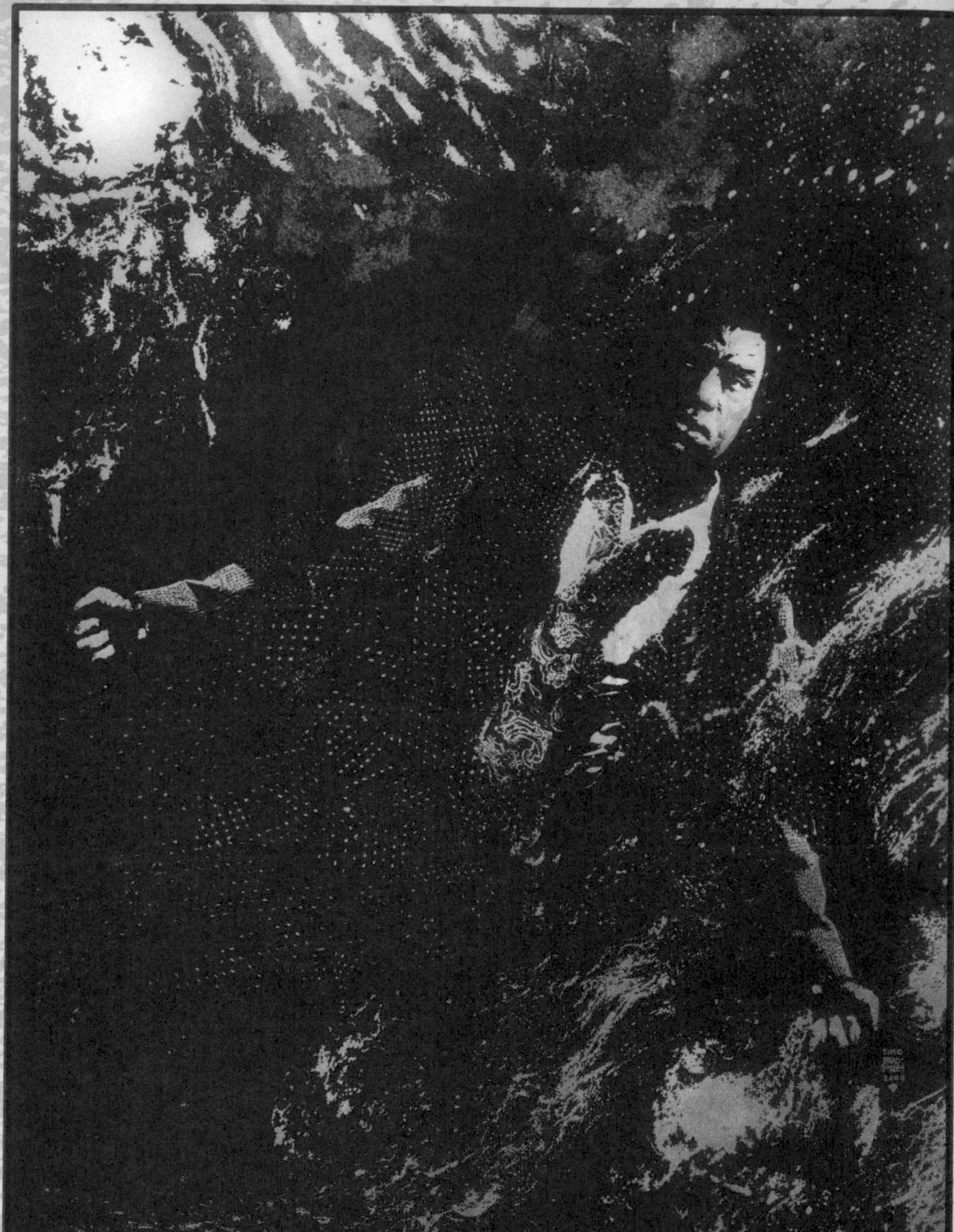

FOUR

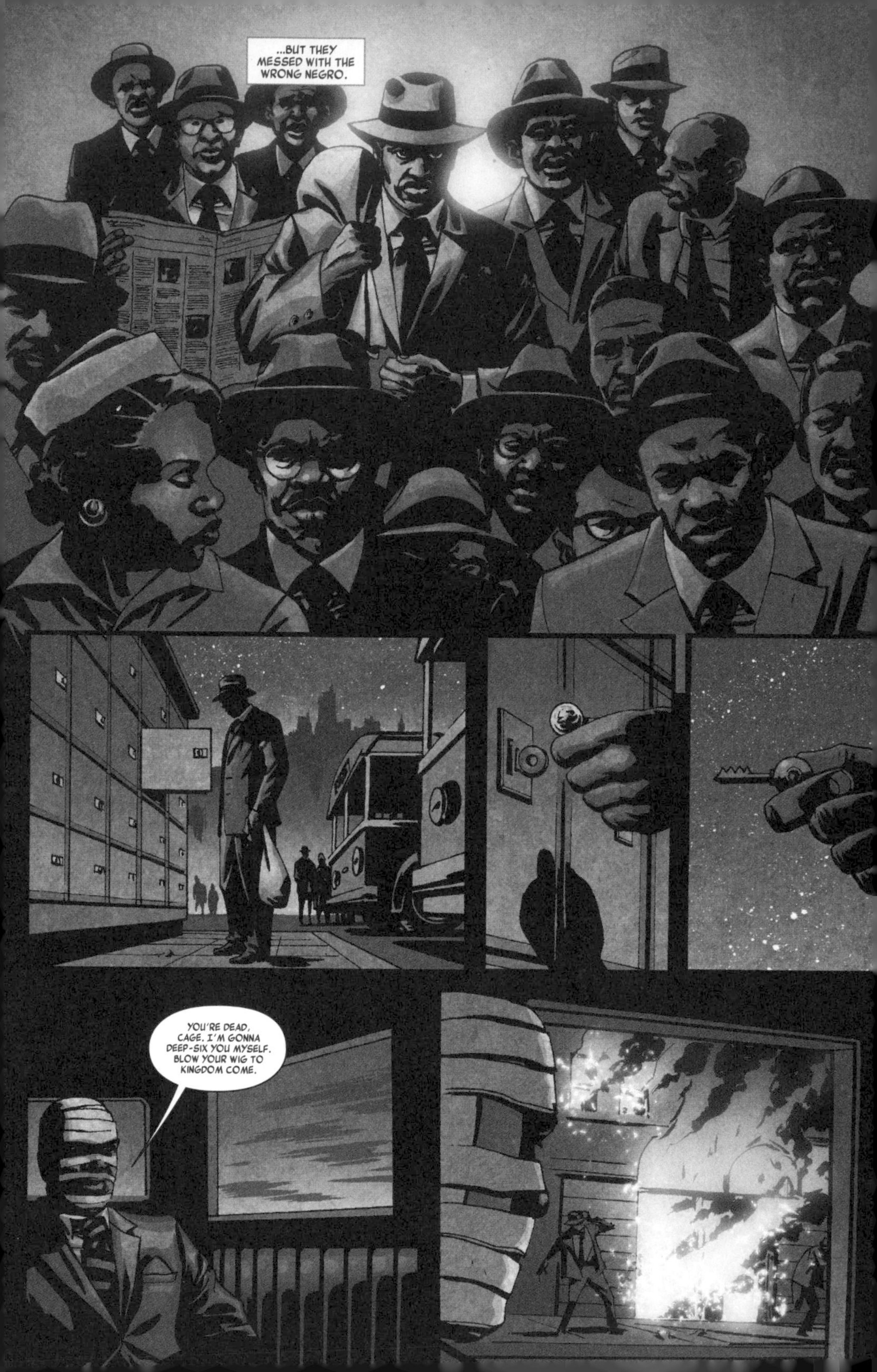
...BUT THEY MESSED WITH THE WRONG NEGRO.
YOU'RE DEAD, CAGE. I'M GONNA DEEP-SIX YOU MYSELF. BLOW YOUR WIG TO KINGDOM COME.

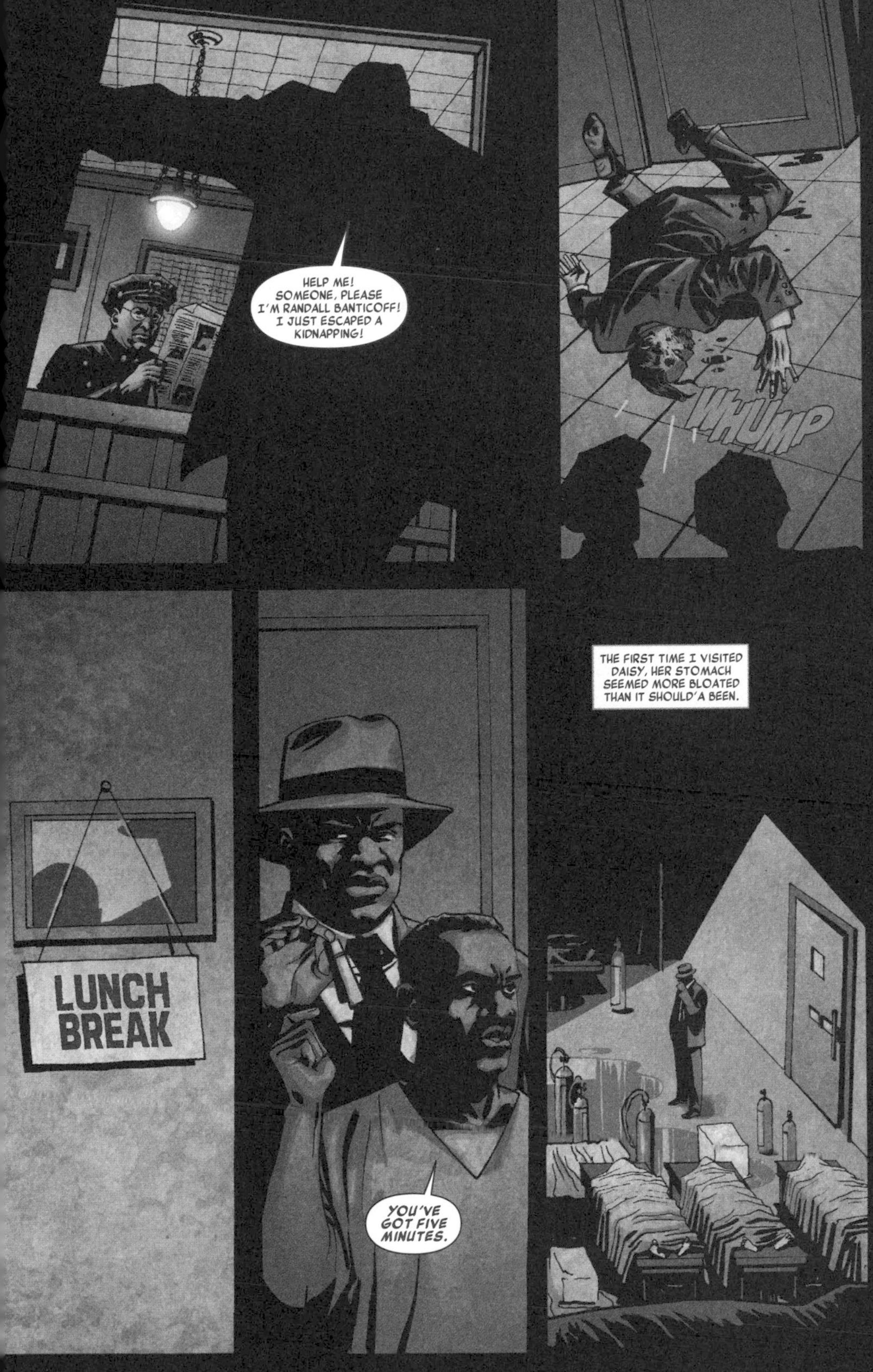
HELP ME! SOMEONE, PLEASE I'M RANDALL BANTICOFF! I JUST ESCAPED A KIDNAPPING!
WHUMP
LUNCH BREAK
YOU'VE GOT FIVE MINUTES.
THE FIRST TIME I VISITED DAISY, HER STOMACH SEEMED MORE BLOATED THAN IT SHOULD'A BEEN.

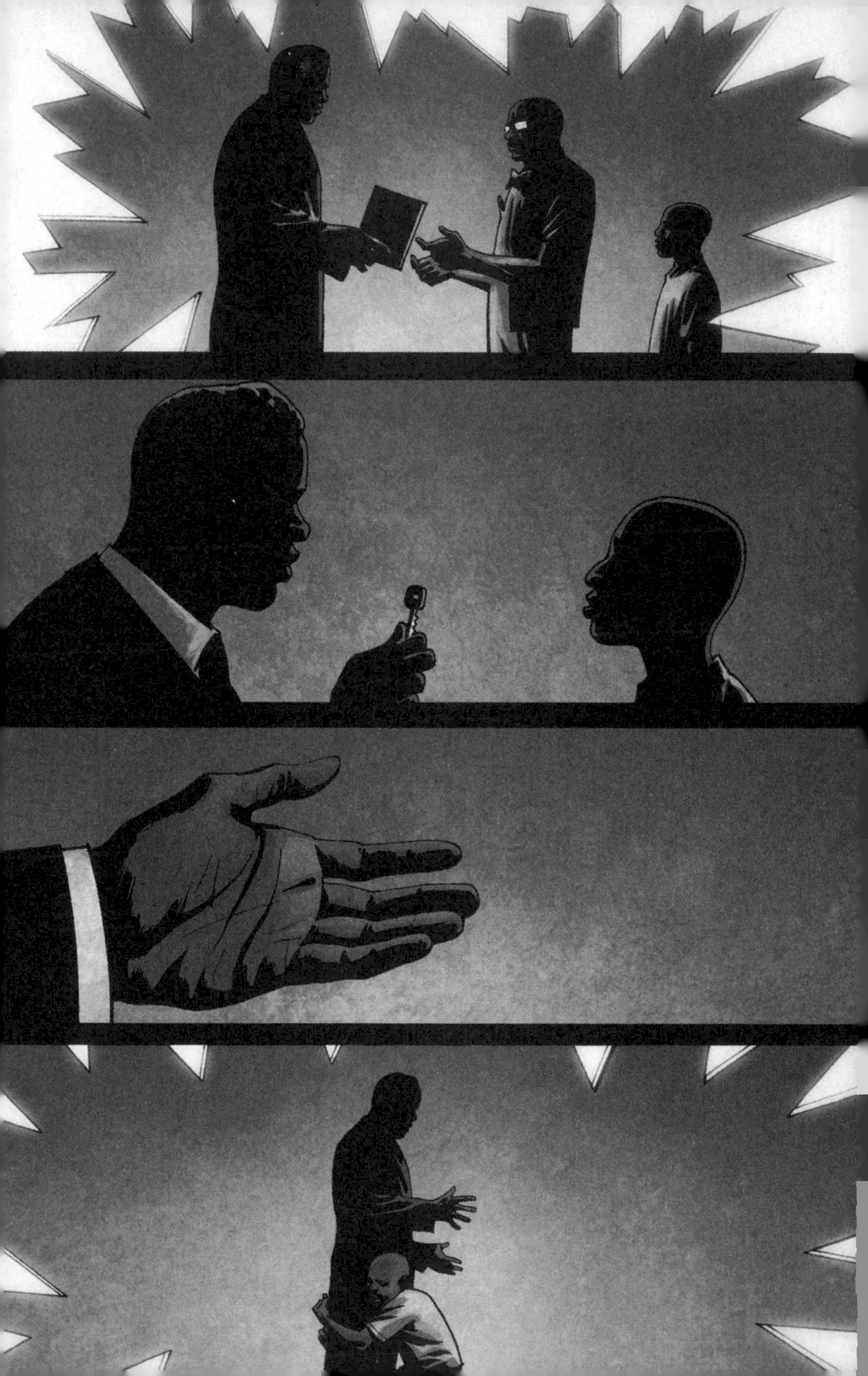

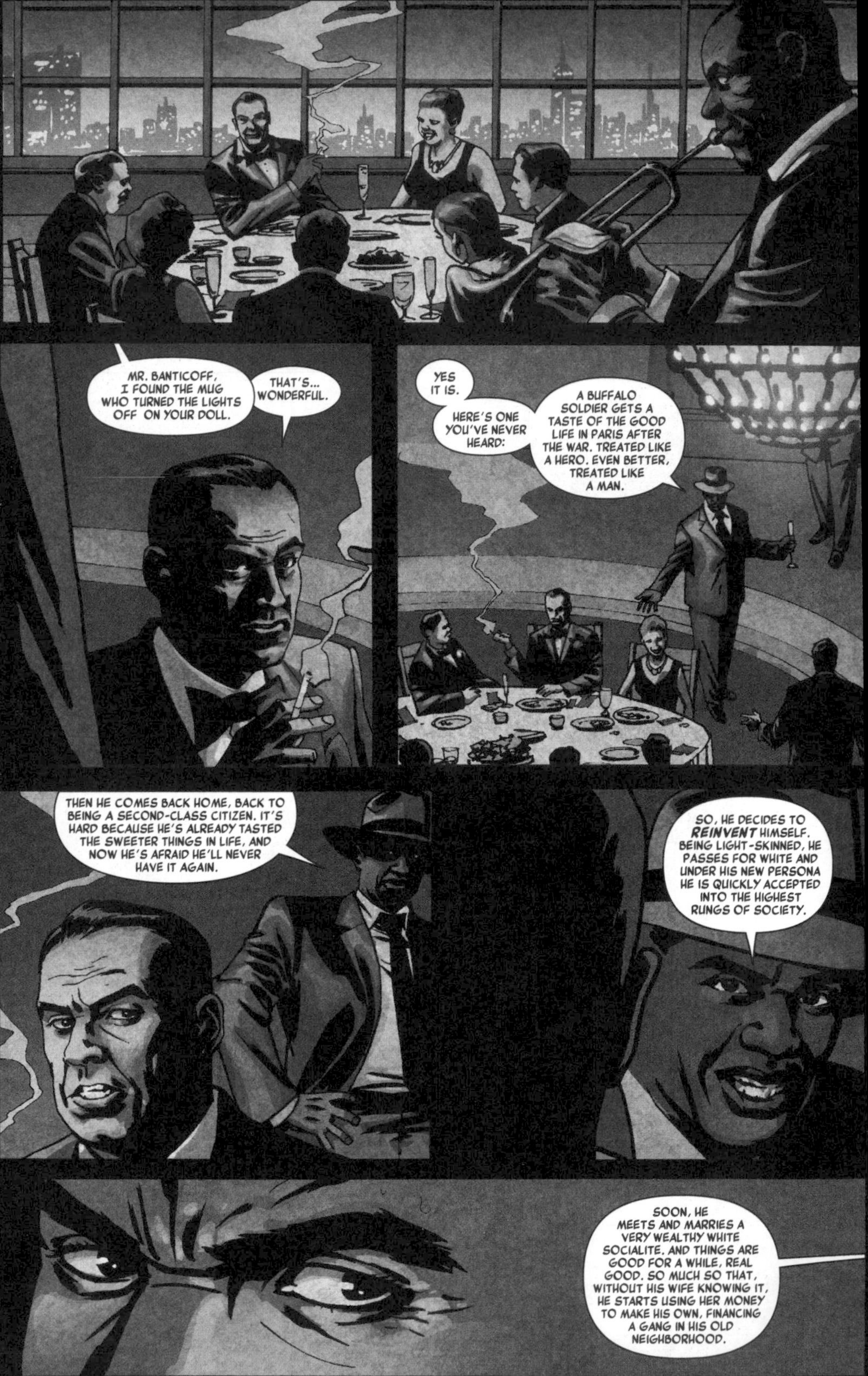
MR. BANTICOFF, I FOUND THE MUG WHO TURNED THE LIGHTS OFF ON YOUR DOLL.
THAT'S... WONDERFUL.
YES IT IS.
HERE'S ONE YOU'VE NEVER HEARD:
A BUFFALO SOLDIER GETS A TASTE OF THE GOOD LIFE IN PARIS AFTER THE WAR. TREATED LIKE A HERO. EVEN BETTER, TREATED LIKE A MAN.
THEN HE COMES BACK HOME, BACK TO BEING A SECOND-CLASS CITIZEN. IT'S HARD BECAUSE HE'S ALREADY TASTED THE SWEETER THINGS IN LIFE, AND NOW HE'S AFRAID HE'LL NEVER HAVE IT AGAIN.
SO, HE DECIDES TO REINVENT HIMSELF. BEING LIGHT-SKINNED, HE PASSES FOR WHITE AND UNDER HIS NEW PERSONA HE IS QUICKLY ACCEPTED INTO THE HIGHEST RUNGS OF SOCIETY.
SOON, HE MEETS AND MARRIES A VERY WEALTHY WHITE SOCIALITE. AND THINGS ARE GOOD FOR A WHILE, REAL GOOD. SO MUCH SO THAT, WITHOUT HIS WIFE KNOWING IT, HE STARTS USING HER MONEY TO MAKE HIS OWN, FINANCING A GANG IN HIS OLD NEIGHBORHOOD.

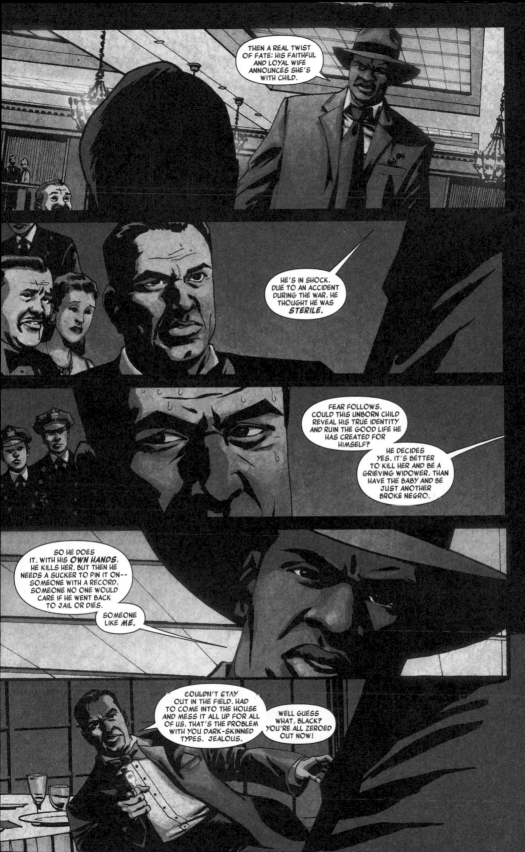

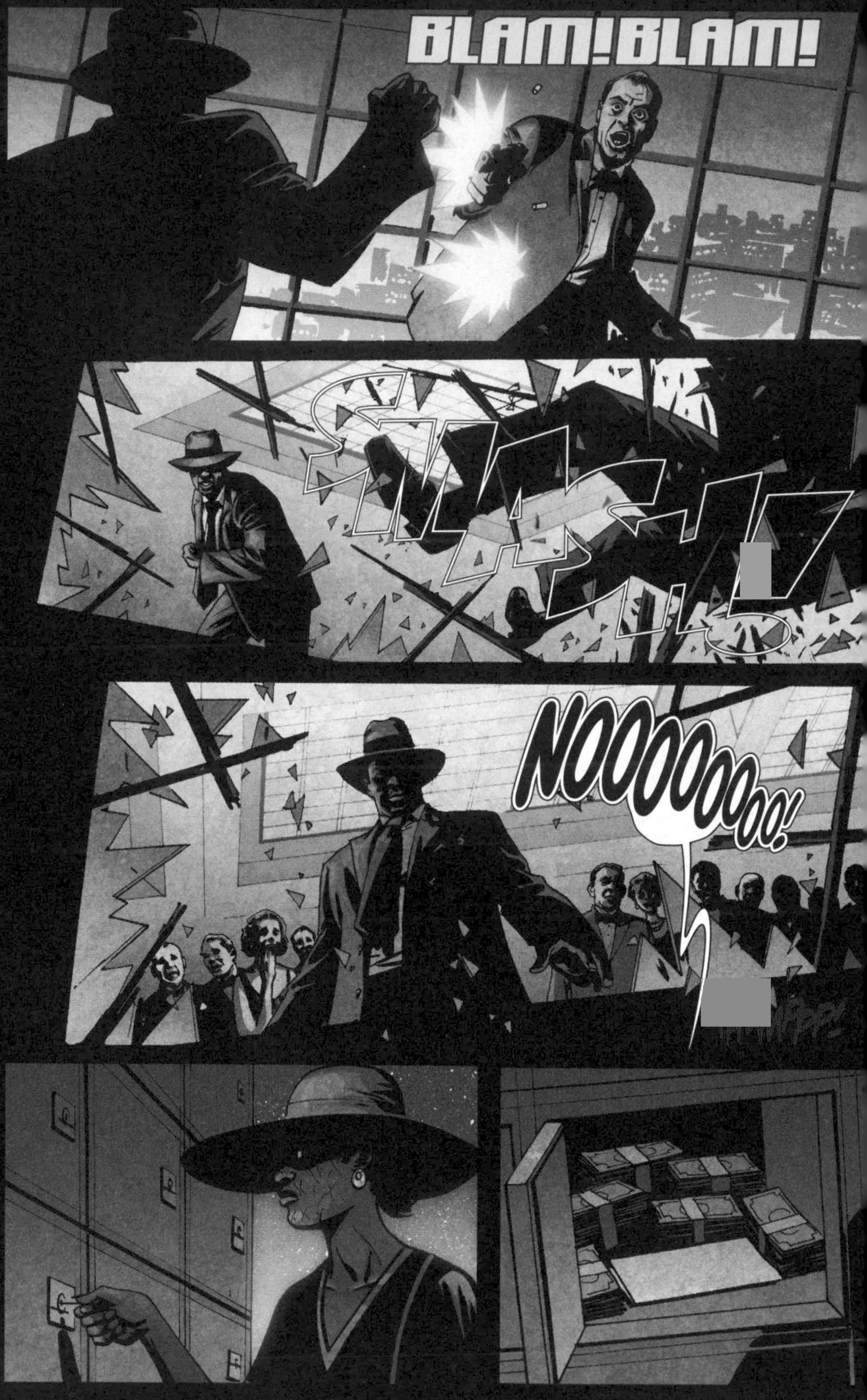
BLAM!BLAM!
NOOOOOOOOO!

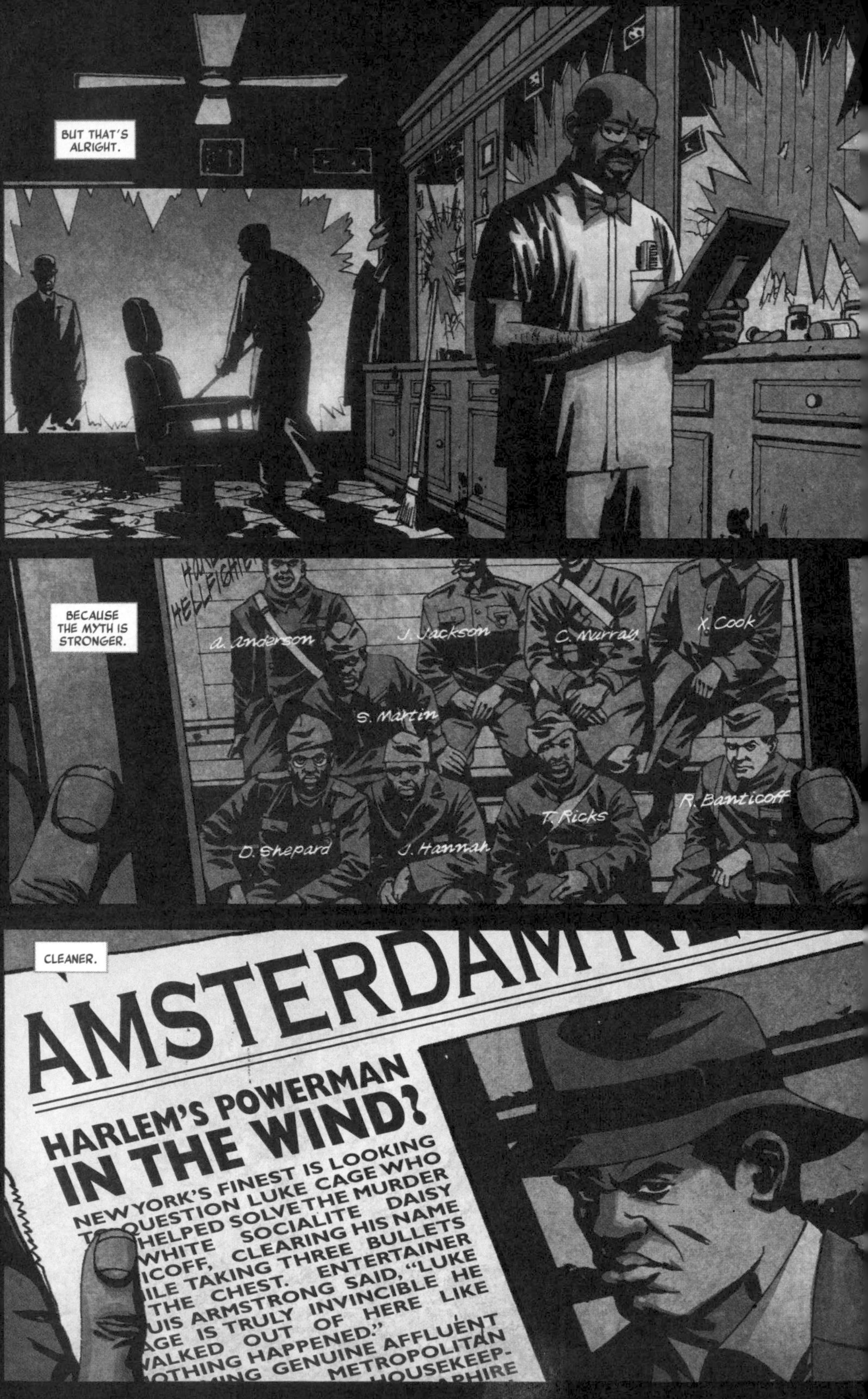

BUT THAT'S ALRIGHT.
BECAUSE THE MYTH IS STRONGER.
HELLFIGHTERS
A. Anderson
J. Jackson
C. Murray
X. Cook
S. Martin
D. Shepard
J. Hannah
T. Ricks
R. Banticoff
CLEANER.
AMSTERDAM
HARLEM'S POWERMAN
IN THE WIND?
NEW YORK'S FINEST IS LOOKING
QUESTION LUKE CAGE WHO
HELPED SOLVE THE MURDER
WHITE SOCIALITE DAISY
ICOFF, CLEARING HIS NAME
ILE TAKING THREE BULLETS
THE CHEST. ENTERTAINER
UIS ARMSTRONG SAID, "LUKE
AGE IS TRULY INVINCIBLE HE
WALKED OUT OF HERE LIKE
OTHING HAPPENED."
AFFLUENT
GENUINE METROPOLITAN
HOUSEKEEP-

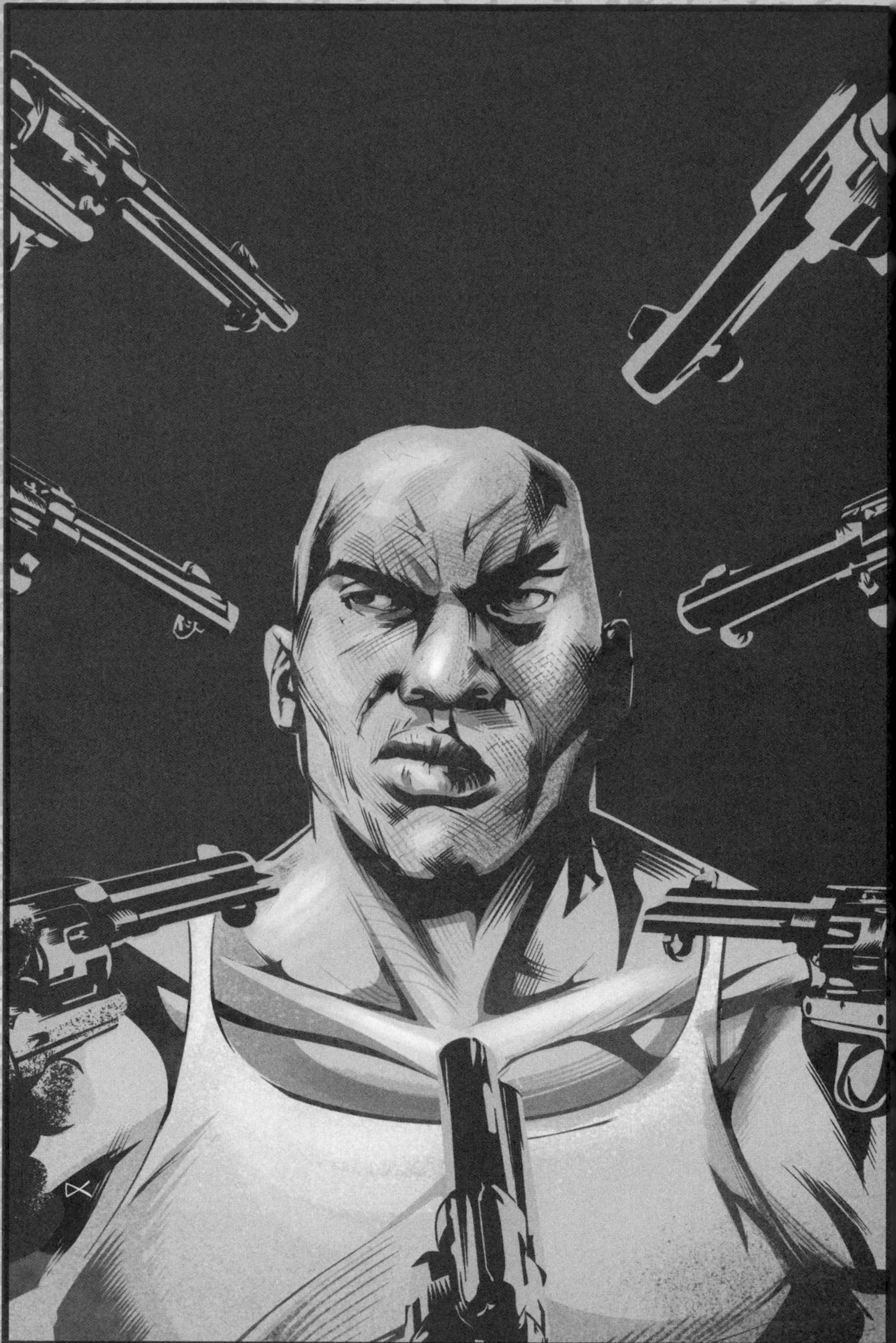

#1 VARIANT BY DENNIS CALERO

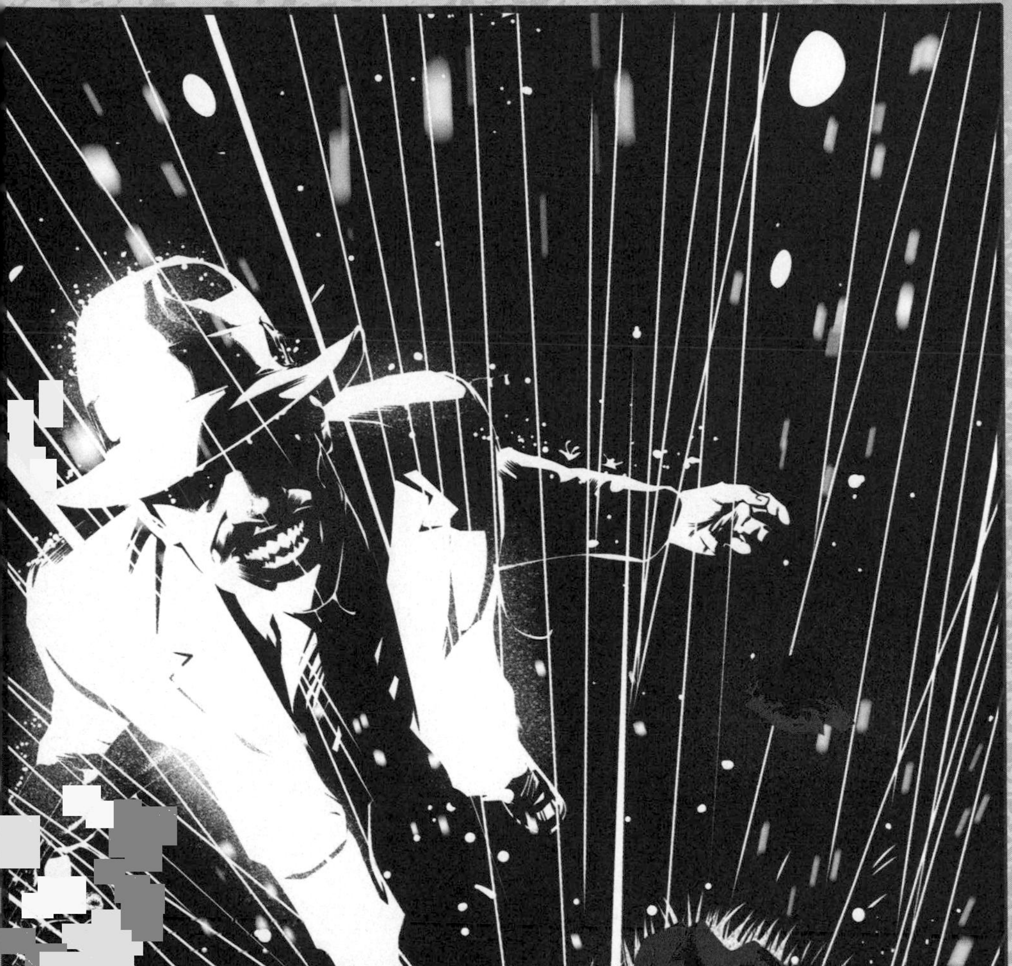

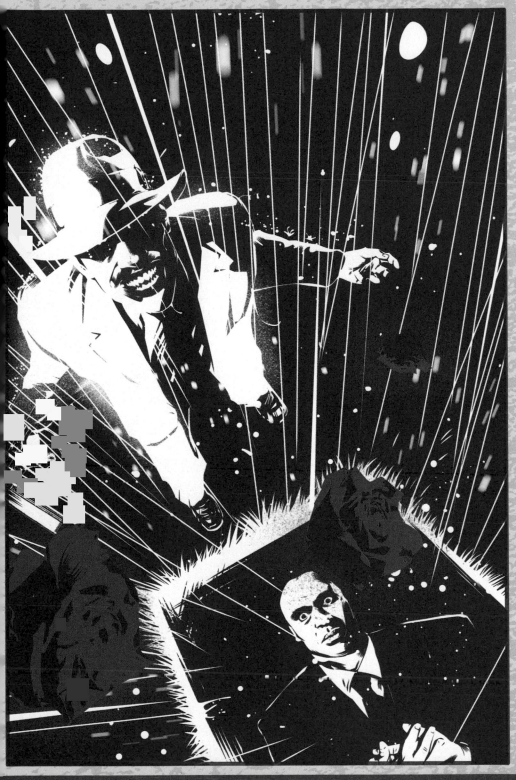

#2 VARIANT BY DENNIS CALERO

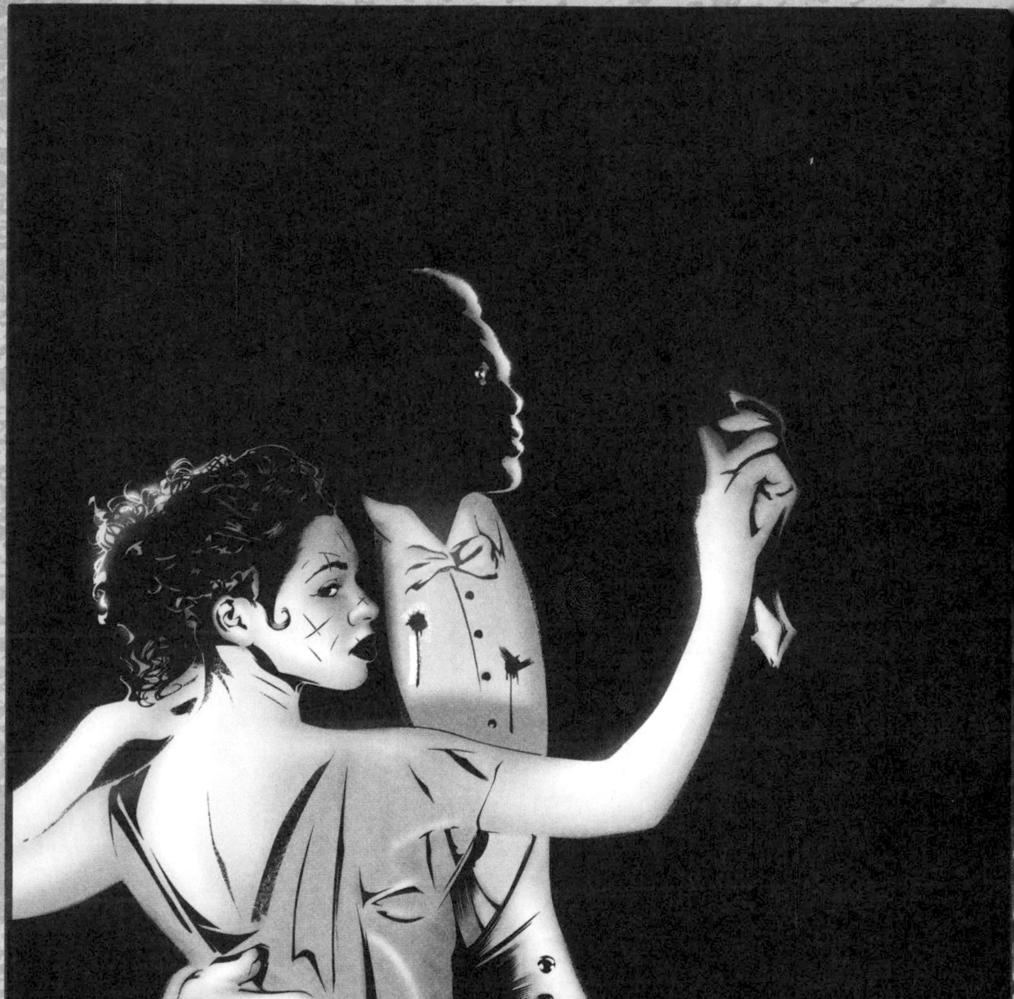

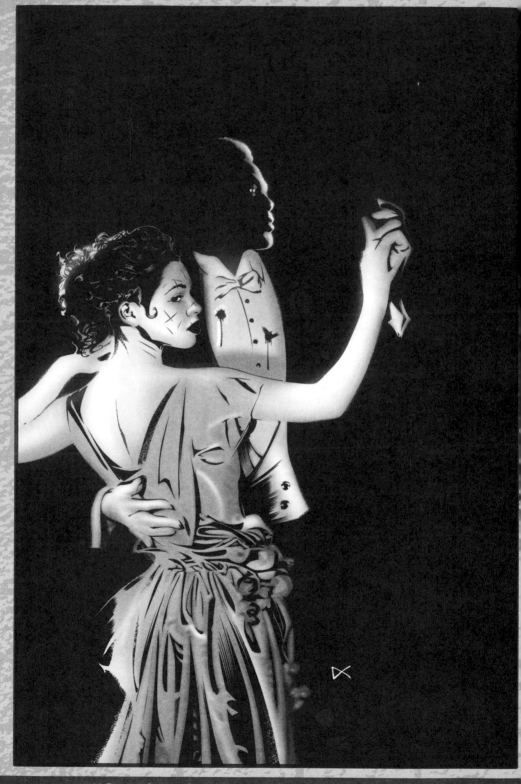

#3 VARIANT BY DENNIS CALERO

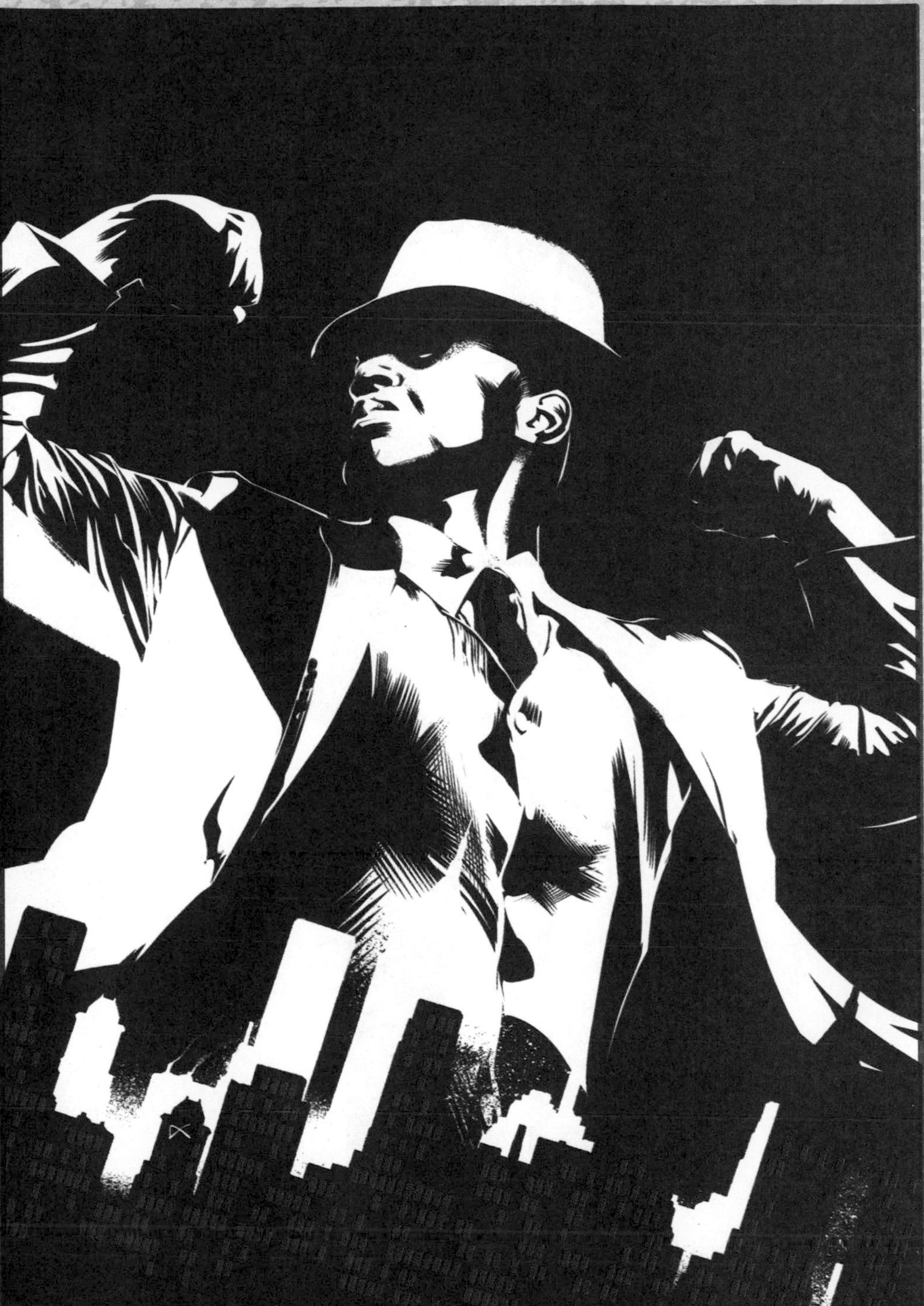

#4 VARIANT BY DENNIS CALERO

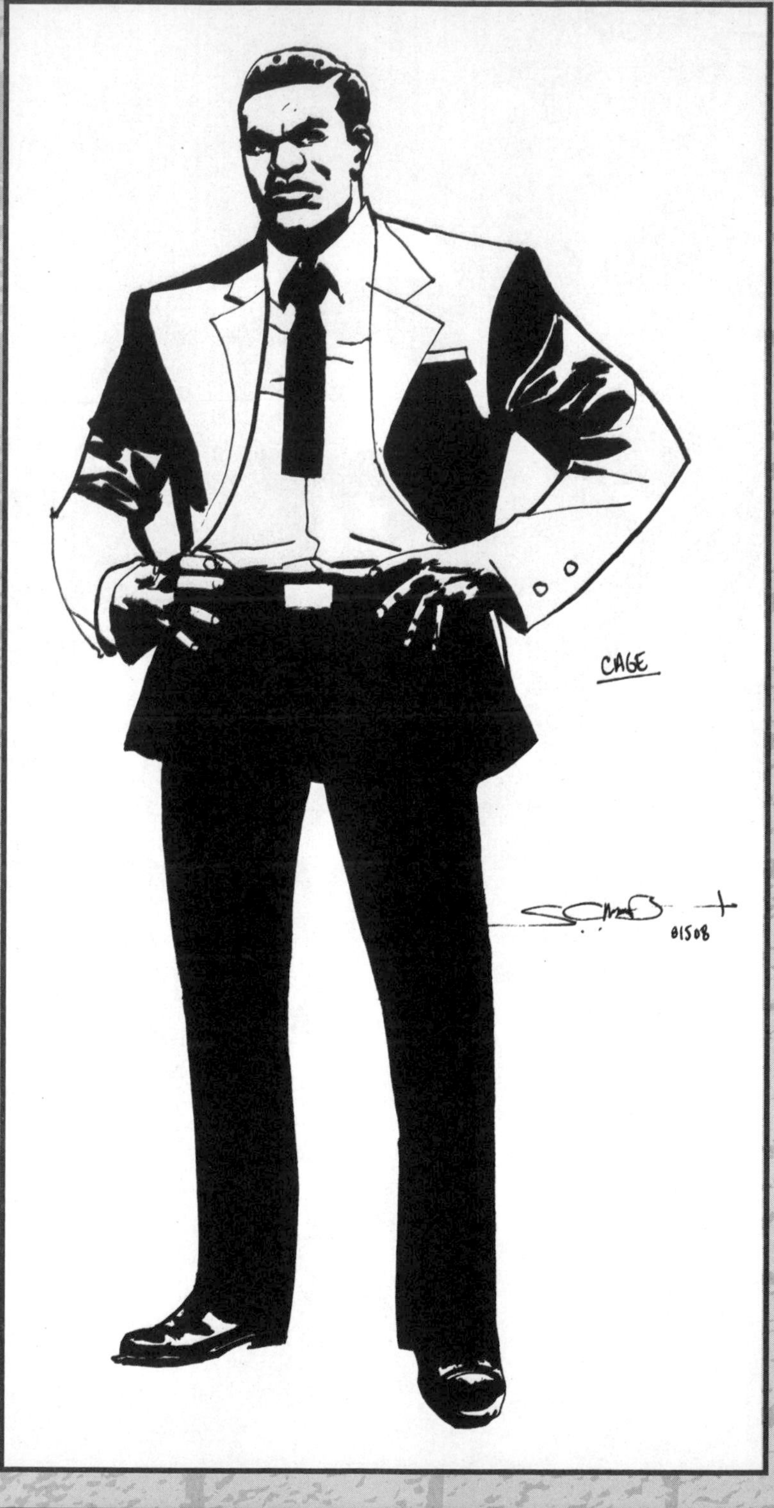
CAGE

CONCEPT ART BY SHAWN MARTINBROUGH

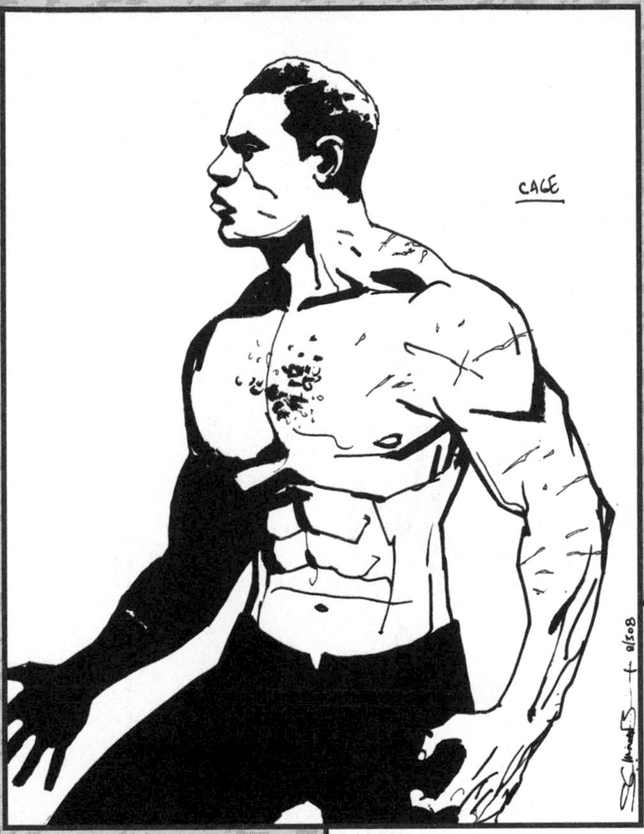
CAGE

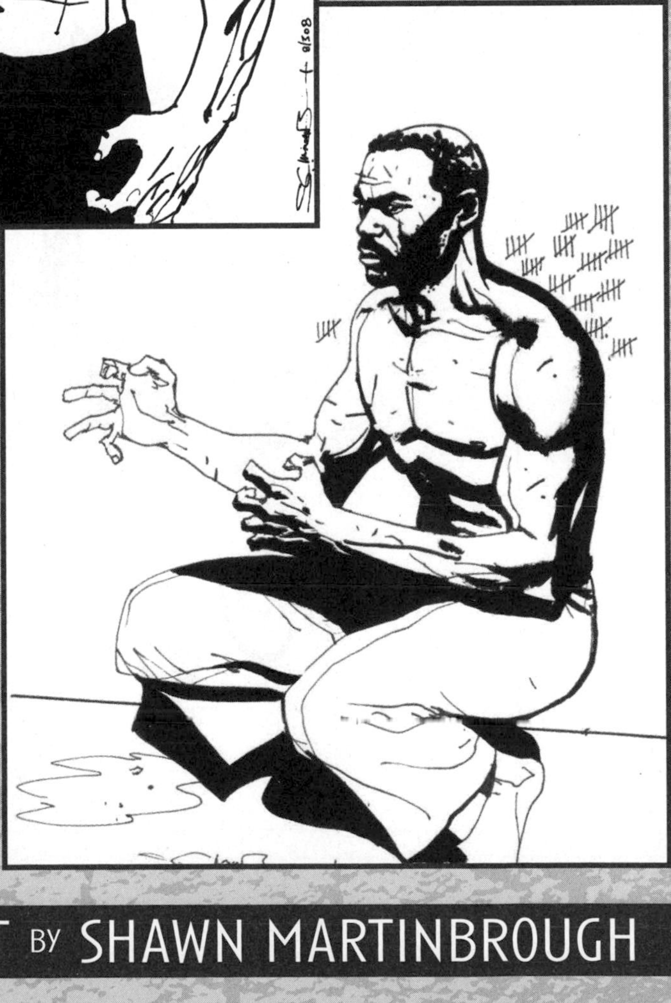

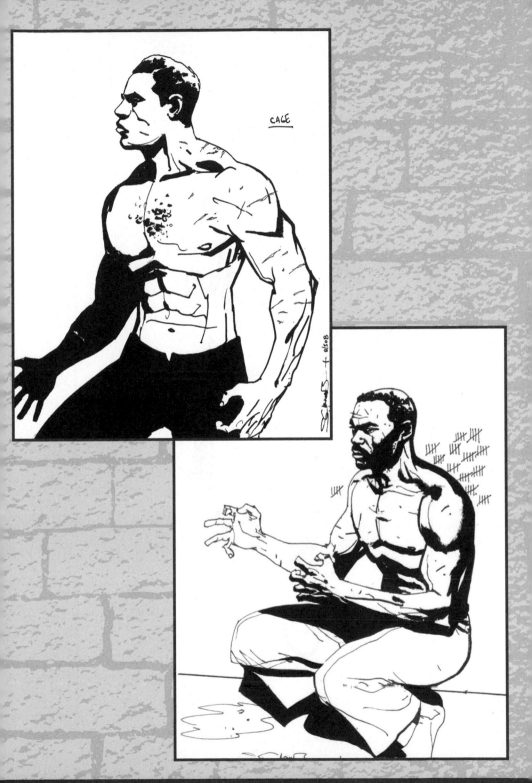

CONCEPT ART BY SHAWN MARTINBROUGH

JOSEPHINE
BALL

81408

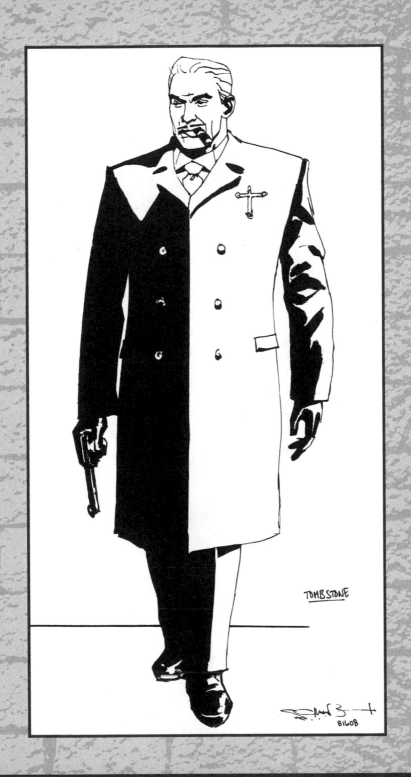

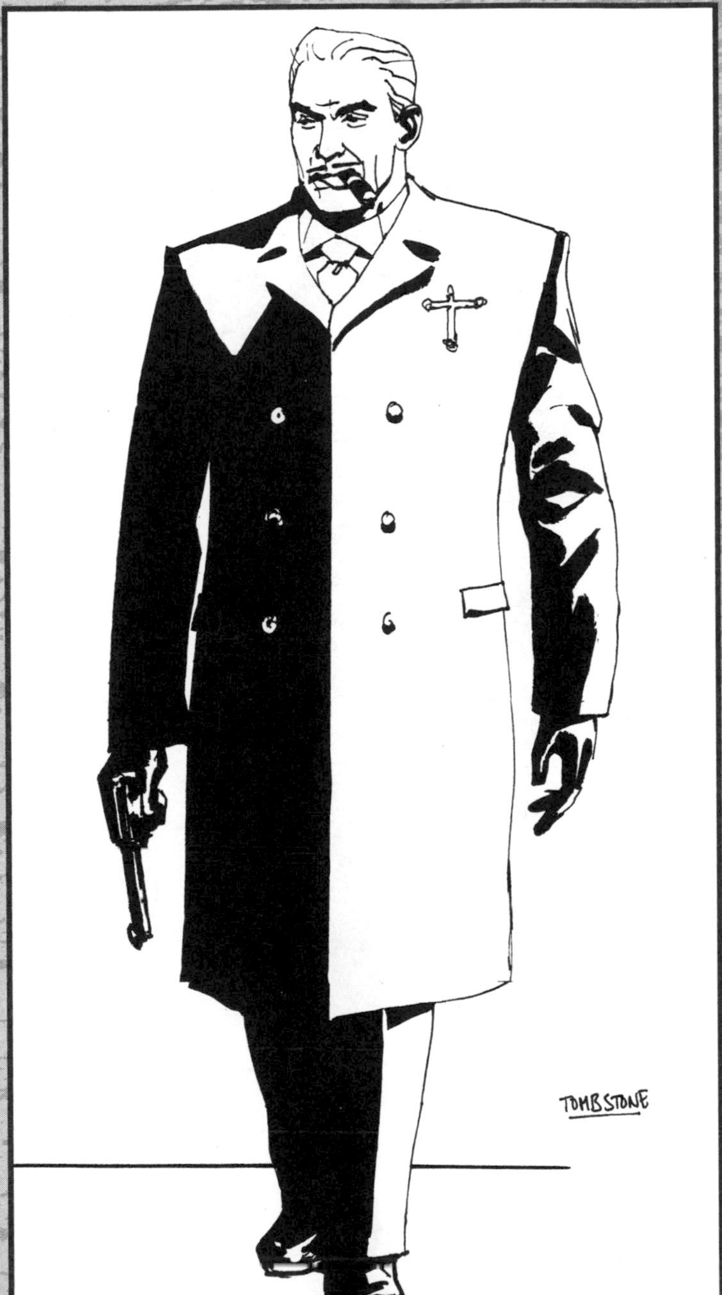
TOMBSTONE
81608

CONCEPT ART BY SHAWN MARTINBROUGH

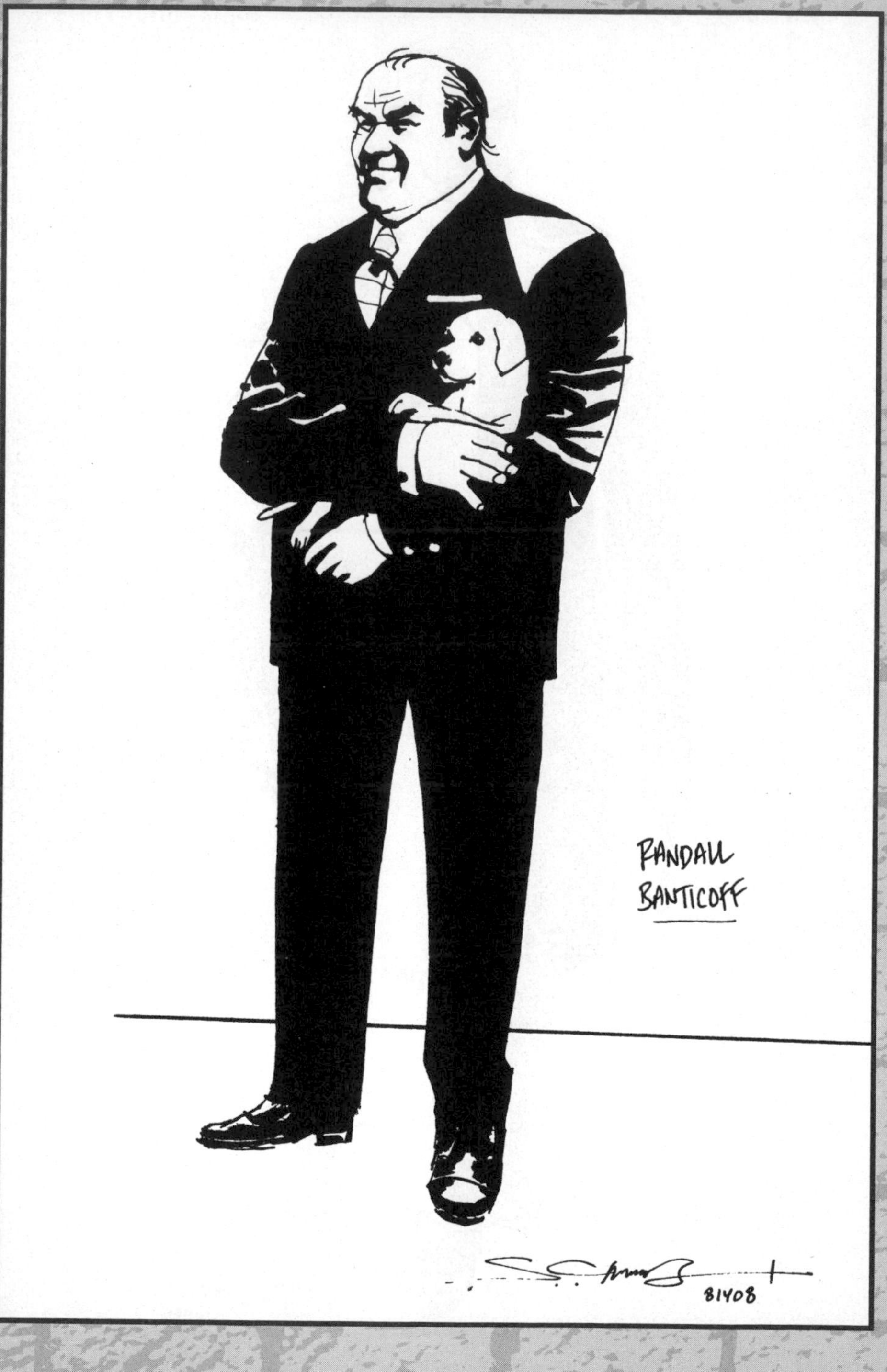
RANDALL
BANTICOFF
81408

CONCEPT ART BY SHAWN MARTINBROUGH

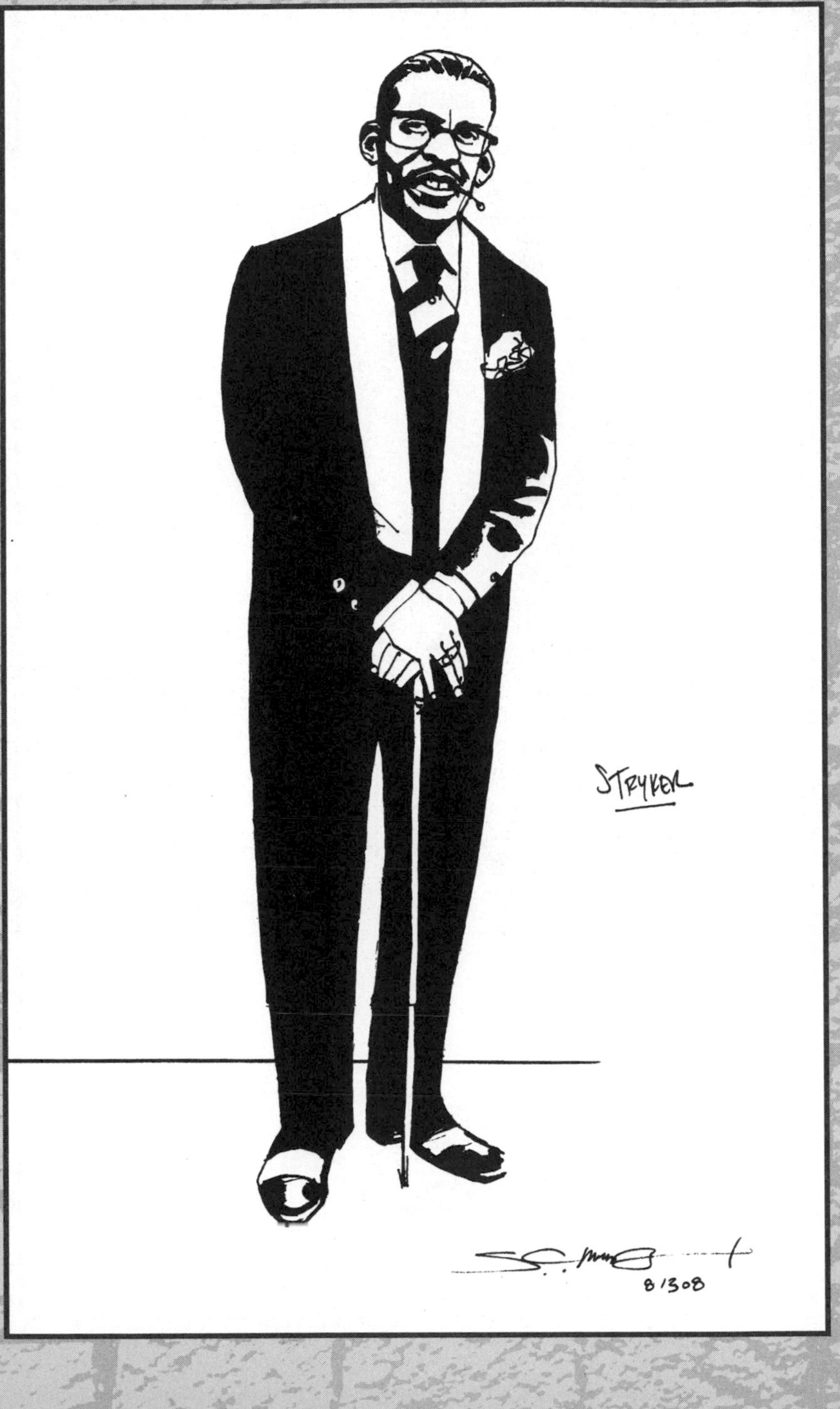
STRYKER
8/30/08

CONCEPT ART BY SHAWN MARTINBROUGH

CONCEPT ART BY SHAWN MARTINBROUGH

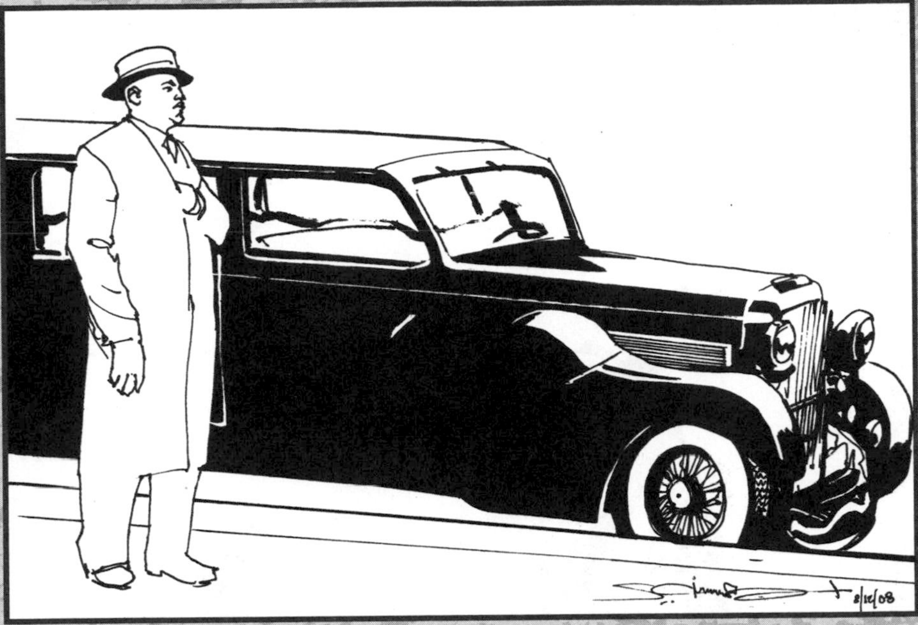

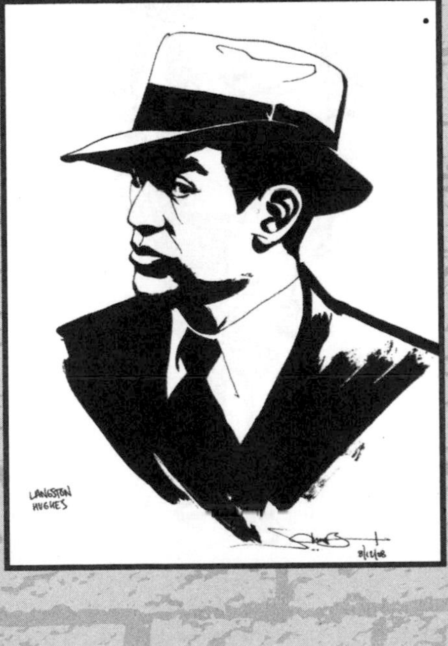
LANGSTON HUGHES

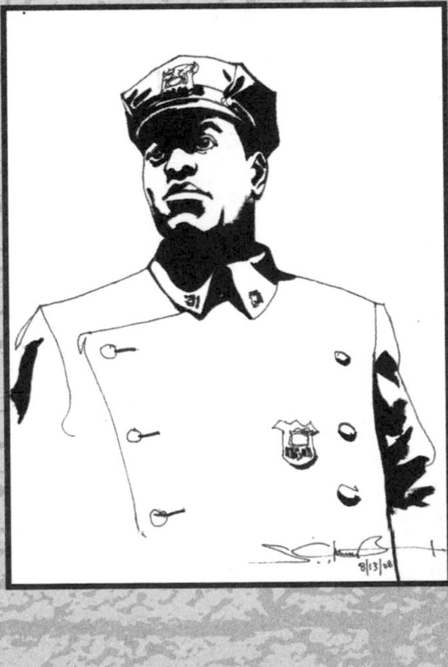

CONCEPT ART BY SHAWN MARTINBROUGH

CONCEPT ART BY SHAWN MARTINBROUGH